Worth Travelling Miles to See

Worth Travelling Miles to See

DIARY OF A SURVEY TRIP TO LAKE TEMISKAMING, 1886

A.H. TELFER

Edited by Lorene DiCorpo

Natural Heritage Books
Toronto

Published by Natural Heritage / Natural History Inc.
P.O. Box 95, Station O, Toronto, Ontario M4A 2M8
www.naturalheritagebooks.com

National Library of Canada Cataloguing in Publication

Telfer, A. H. (Alexander Herkes), 1832-1911
    Worth travelling miles to see : diary of a survey trip to Lake Temiskaming, 1886 / A.H. Telfer ; edited by Lorene DiCorpo.

Includes bibliographical references and index.
ISBN 1-896219-87-X

1. Telfer, A. H. (Alexander Herkes), 1832-1911—Diaries. 2. Surveyors—Ontario—Diaries. 3. Surveying—Timiskaming, Lake, Region (Ont. and Quebec) 4. Timiskaming, Lake, Region (Ont. and Quebec)—Description and travel. I. DiCorpo, Lorene, 1943- II. Title.

FC3067.3.T44 2004   917.13'144   C2003-903576-X

Front cover illustrations: top: *Courtesy of the Archives of Ontario, Jones Collection, C147-1-0-1-4 (AO 4589)*; Middle left: *Courtesy of the Canadian Pacific Archives, A.17135*; Middle right: *Courtesy of the Haliburton Highlands Museum*; Bottom: *Courtesy of the Archives of Ontario, Jones Collection, C147-1-0-1-2 (AO 4588)*.
Back cover illustrations: Top: *Courtesy of Lorene DiCorpo*; Bottom: *Courtesy of Chris Oslond, Curator, Haileybury Heritage Museum*.

Cover and text design by Sari Naworynski
Edited by Jane Gibson
Printed and bound in Canada by Hignell Book Printing, Winnipeg

Natural Heritage / Natural History Inc. acknowledges the financial support of the Canada Council for the Arts and the Ontario Arts Council for our publishing program. We acknowledge the support of the Government of Ontario through the Ontario Media Development Corporation's Ontario Book Initiative. We also acknowledge the financial support of the Government of Canada through the Book Publishing Industry Development Program (BPIDP) and the Association for the Export of Canadian Books.

Dedication

For my mother, Irene Telfer Laycock, and my uncle,
William Harvey Telfer,
"The Romford Hill Mob" of the northern hamlet
of Romford, Ontario

*"Ah, but a man's reach should exceed his grasp,
Or what's a heaven for?"*
— ROBERT BROWNING [1]

Contents

Acknowledgements

Many people have been instrumental in bringing this book into being. First, I am thankful for my mother's vision and determination to make the diary story a reality. I would also like to thank my publisher Barry Penhale for believing in the project and sharing with me an interest in the history of the Temiskaming area; and Dr. Scott Moir of the Scottish Studies Department, University of Guelph, for encouraging me to develop the original concept in the context of Scottish contributions to Canada. Staff members at the Archives of Ontario and the Ministry of Natural Resources were both helpful and patient as I searched for historical data and appropriate visual material. I am especially grateful to Reference Archivist Christine Bourolias for her guidance in using the resources in Special Collections, and to Al Day, Crown Lands Survey Clerk, for giving me access to "the vaults" of old survey records. The curators of Ontario heritage museums I visited were very supportive. Chris Oslund of Haileybury Heritage Museum and Tom Ballantyne of Haliburton Highlands Museum generously provided me with photographs, and Gerard Therrien of Mattawa and District Museum shared his manuscript-in-progress of Mattawa's history. In dealing with the history of surveying in Ontario, Mr. John Quinsey, OLS (ret.) kindly directed me to the search tools he had created at the Archives of Ontario.

Much appreciation goes to genealogist, historian and author Bruce W. Taylor of New Liskeard, who has provided valuable insights into the history of the period by giving permission to use generous excerpts from his previous works. These excerpts are found in the Notes section of this book.

Finally, I must thank my family and my husband Nick, for their enthusiastic support and companionship on this journey.

The support and suggestions from so many have been invaluable, but in the final analysis, I, as editor and compiler of the material, am the one responsible for the accuracy of this material. Any issues brought to my attention or to the publisher will be addressed in subsequent editions.

Preface

My grandfather's shed always fascinated me. It was a treasure trove of vintage clothing, bush camping accessories and family mementos and, in particular, an old Victorian school desk whose contents were reverently referred to as "the old books from Scotland." The antiquity of some of these volumes left me in awe – more so than the collection of pocket-size diaries, written in faded pencil by my Scottish great-grandfather over 100 years ago as he recounted his adventures as part of a Northern Ontario survey crew. It was my mother who, on a quest for genealogical information, drew my attention to the narrative contained in these little diaries, and suggested I should use them as the basis for a book. Having read Susannah Moodie's and Mrs. Simcoe's accounts of pioneer life, she was convinced that this story too was worth sharing!

Events of the diary begin with departure from Toronto in July of 1886 and a journey by rail to Mattawa, where the entire survey crew assembled. Transport was then by steamer and portage up the Ottawa River to Lake Temiskaming. Starting at the northern boundary of Lorraine township in the District of Nipissing (surveyed the previous year) the crew proceeded to run lines for seven more townships up the west side of the lake, ending at the northeast corner near the mouth of the Blanche River; all the while accompanied by the hazards of mud, flies, cold, fatigue and multiple physical dangers. A.H. Telfer's diary concludes, after a parting of ways by the crew at Mattawa, as he makes his way alone southward via the Muskoka Junction Railway and on foot back to York Mills. Although enthusiasm for the adventure and wry humour are evident, a sense of melancholy and longing for family back home pervades the writing. These rich sensory images and contrasts, and the feelings evoked by them, drew me into the story and gave me the incentive to share it with others.

Upon retirement from my teaching career, I decided to take my mother's challenge seriously, and embarked on the "diary project," as it had become known. Numerous trips to the towns of the Nipissing and Temiskaming areas, their museums and excursions on the Polar Bear Express and Temiskaming Timber Train, all provided a rich context for the research that followed. Most of the background data was to come from the Archives of Ontario, where I spent many hours perusing reels of microfilm, fragile maps and old photo collections. I was also in contact with the CP's Corporate Archives in Montreal, and with the MNR Information branch where I was able to access Alexander Niven's hand-drawn survey maps and field notes.

As I immersed myself in the project, I met many interesting people with a passion for history, who encouraged me to share this story. Although the diary poignantly speaks for itself, I have chosen to add, through the introduction and endnotes, my own editorial voice. The diary itself is presented as the original. No attempt has been made to correct any spellings (or their variations). But, for consistency, the spellings "Temiskaming" and "Niven," have been used throughout the editor's Historical Overview. From time to time a clarification phrase or word has been inserted.

PART ONE

Historical Overview

Alexander Herkes Telfer: Spirit of the Pioneer

Alexander Herkes Telfer was born in the Parish of Rogart, County Sutherland, Scotland, on November 21, 1832, in the midst of what historians have called "the emigration century." His parents, Andrew Telfer and Janet Herkes, along with some of their relatives, joined the tide of emigrants heading to the North American colonies in 1833.[1] Several factors could have influenced their decision to leave, including the cholera epidemic of 1832, which had swept mercilessly through Britain. As genteel but poor crofters, they foresaw only harder economic times to come from the amalgamation of properties by the large landholders. It was hoped that a better life for their children would await them in Upper Canada, the destination for increasing numbers of Scots and English. Undaunted by the prospect of twelve weeks at sea and perhaps ignorant of the miseries of steerage accommodation, the Telfers, accompanied by a group of relatives, set sail from

Alexander Herkes Telfer.
The photographer's
credit reads Buckley &
Co., Niagara Falls, Ont.
Courtesy of the Telfer
Family.

Cromarty in June.[2] That Alexander was the only one of their four
children to survive the voyage is a foreshadowing of the resilience
and fortitude of this ordinary yet remarkable man.

The family disembarked at Quebec, where the presence of
cholera was once again evident and likely claimed more lives.[3]
There was little time to mourn; the Telfers continued their journey
up the St. Lawrence, enduring the primitive transport available at
the time, namely bateaux, steamer or stagecoach, and finally made
their way to Upper Canada, settling in Scarborough township, to
the east of York. Once there, the Telfer families acquired property
in the Malvern area and a farm and apple orchard were established.[4] Alexander grew up in and around Agincourt, Malvern,
Woburn and Don Mills, the villages of the Don River watershed.
Despite the tragedies and trials they had experienced in their
travels, the presence of many of their countrymen and women

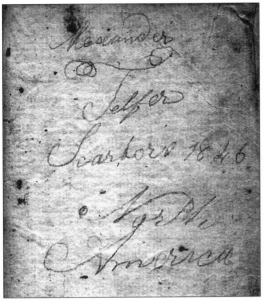

Inscription found in a family collection of books from Scotland, written on an early page in an original 18th-century text. Courtesy of the Telfer Family.

was a comfort. Like many others, they brought their music with them too, and soon Andrew Telfer was in demand as a fiddler at local gatherings. As a further counter to the hardships of pioneer life, religion and education were cornerstones of the family lifestyles. Alexander's parents were founding members of the Knox Presbyterian congregation of Agincourt,[5] and sent their son to the one-room school run by a fellow Scottish emigrant, John Muir.[6] There, Alexander grew in literacy and patriotic spirit, recording in elaborate script in his mother's bible, "Alexander Herkes Telfer, 1846, Scarboro, North America."[7] He was a citizen of the New World.

In 1858, Alexander married Mary Jane Harrington from Scarborough, Ontario, a descendant of pioneers who had emigrated from the United States in the first decade of the nineteenth century. They had seven children whom they raised in Scarborough, and later in York Mills. Not untypical of the times,

Alexander worked at a variety of jobs. In the Census of 1871, his occupation is recorded as Postmaster for District 45, Scarboro. However, ambition always seemed to exceed the realities of making a living, and when the opportunity presented itself to join a survey crew travelling to the northern woods of New Ontario in 1886, it was an opportunity to be embraced.

This survey expedition was led by Alexander Niven from Haliburton, a Public Land Surveyor of considerable experience in the northern districts of the province. In anticipation of submitting a report to the Temiscamingue Settlers' Association, which had an interest in the land being surveyed with a view to purchasing a plot, Alexander H. Telfer kept a vividly detailed diary of the daily events. Although he included the technical data of survey measurement and soil evaluation, it was in the depiction of human experience that he excelled. His letters to his family during that time probably avoided the worst of the hardships he endured, but they provided his loved ones with a window on a world seen by few in the more "civilized" south.

ALEXANDER NIVEN: A LIFE WELL LIVED

When Alexander Niven passed away in the Victoria Hospital, Toronto, on May 7, 1911, an accomplished career in land surveying came to a close. During his years of public service, toiling in the bush land of Ontario, he left a wealth of cartographic information and data that remains a standard reference today.

Born at Niagara-on-the-Lake, Ontario, on October 14, 1836, he was one of five children of Robert Niven and Ann Morrison, Scottish immigrants from Perthshire. While his brother David studied for the Presbyterian ministry, Alexander followed up his

Alexander Niven, Registered Land Surveyor, 8th July, 1859. Courtesy of the Archives of Ontario. Lib. Period. Association of Ontario Land Surveyors Annual Report, 1911.

Niagara Grammar School education with studies in land surveying at Toronto, passing examinations as a Provincial Land Surveyor in 1859. In the same year, he began his practice in the village of St. Mary's in Oxford County, Ontario. It was during this time that he likely made a first acquaintance with his future wife, Maggie McEvoy.

In 1868, Alexander Niven's career shifted in a somewhat different direction. A group of English entrepreneurs under the chairmanship of the Honourable Thomas Chandler Haliburton,[8] a former Chief Justice of Nova Scotia, had formed the Canadian Land & Emigration Company (CL&E),[9] and were looking for an agent to survey lots, prepare purchase agreements and assess timber to be harvested on company land. The CL&E had purchased a block of townships in the area now known as Hailburton[10] with a view to developing and selling the land for settlement. This was a rather incongruous plan, considering that the government had been issuing free land grants for some time, yet the company believed that providing assistance to settlers was a worthy cause that would be rewarded. Besides, the Canada Company had been selling land for settlement in the Huron Tract since the early 1830s.[11] Niven was offered the grand sum of $1,000 per annum plus 5% commission on all sales of land completed during the year. He countered with an offer of $1,200, which was accepted. Thus began his ten-year association with the CL&E. It was an up and down relationship, but no one could fault Niven for his rigorous attention to duty. Except for a brief sojurn to marry Miss McEvoy, he worked diligently in the service of company and community, exploring pine stands, preparing a plan of the municipality of Dysart, serving as warden of the county and promoting the extension of the Victoria Railway from Lindsay to Haliburton in 1878.

Although the town of Haliburton would remain his home base, Alexander Niven spent the rest of his career in the employ of T.B. Pardee, the Provincial Commissioner of Crown Lands. The coming of the Canadian Pacific Railway (CPR) aroused great interest in the settlement of the north, and the government hastened to lay out townships near this main transport route. Niven was soon busy in the area north of the French River, moving into the present-day Sudbury district and eventually following the rail line into the Rainy River district. There, over a period of seven years, he ran many base and meridian lines.[12] However, it was in 1881 that he began exploration and running of base lines north of Lake Nipissing into Temiskaming and beyond and, in 1886, he employed A.H. Telfer and some associates from his Haliburton

Alexander Niven, to the right. Early days in Haliburton. Courtesy of the Haliburton Highlands Museum.

days (the Heard brothers and the Native, Bernard)[13] as part of his survey crew to outline seven townships at the head of Lake Temiskaming.[14] Some ten years later, at the age of sixty, Niven was commissioned to run an exploration line extending the Algoma-Sudbury district boundary north to James Bay. It was monumental undertaking of some 300 miles through forest, swamp, clay belt and muskeg, while enduring the flies and vagaries of weather. His efforts earned him historic recognition as this line was later named Niven's Meridian.[15]

Alexander Niven won the respect of his colleagues for his experience and accomplishments. He was a charter member and former president of the Association of Ontario Land Surveyors. Yet in the biographical sketch published by the AOLS at the time of his death, his human qualities also stand out, he was "noted for his management of men," a man who "accomplished things without show" who attested that "his health and strength improved each year on returning to the bush."[16] He was, indeed, one of Ontario's pathfinders.

TEMISKAMING: THE LAND

Prior to the survey of the Temiskaming portion of the Nipissing district, the richness and variety of the land was an unknown quantity, familiar only to the Native Peoples and the few hardy white men who sought out the wilderness. The early trappers and fur traders who followed the ancient waterways and portages established by the Cree, Algonkian and Ojibwa were voyageurs, not colonists. It is interesting to note, though, that one of the early explorations into the area by the Chevalier de Troyes in 1686 for the purpose of protecting French trading interests, was extended to a search for a supposed mine along the west shore of Lake Temiskaming. Although some hard yellow metal samples were brought back, the fur trading network was of primary importance. Over the next hundred years, the area continued to be a source of rivalry and dispute for both the French and English as they pursued their interests in the region and northwards.[17] These men were very well-versed in the ways of the land, but only periodic visitors to the "civilization" offered by the Hudson's Bay Company (HBC) posts such as Fort Temiskaming.[18]

When Alexander Niven's survey party completed the outline of the townships at the head of the lake, the men returned with reports full of glowing endorsements. Niven himself remarked that "There is not in my opinion the equal of this tract of land

The head of this pond marked the beginning of the three La Vase portages, connecting Trout Lake and the lower La Vase River. Using these connections between small ponds and streams, travellers of the great canoe route made their way to the upper Great Lakes and the West. Courtesy of Lorene DiCorpo.

now left in Ontario for settlement."[19] Alexander H. Telfer, one of his crew, added his own observations in a report to the Temiskaming Settlers' Association: "It should offer inducements to the intending settler and young men of Ontario, at least equal to those held out by Manitoba and the North West; as it is nearer home and the great market centres, and there is room for many thousands of homesteads free from rock or stone..."[20]

The Temiskaming district is one of contrasts. It includes those lands of Ontario and Quebec lying west and east of the borders of

Above: View of Beauchene Creek and the Ottawa River from the trestle bridge of the former CPR *"Moccasin Line" to Temiskaming, mile 40.* Courtesy of Lorene DiCorpo.

Below: Some parts of the shore of Lake Temiskaming are dramatic examples of castellated rock. Courtesy of the Archives of Ontario, Jones Collection, C147-3-0-3.

Lake Temiskaming, all part of the large, saucer-shaped Canadian Shield. In the southern part of this area, the rocky outcroppings of the Shield are evident, and those travelling up the Ottawa River to the lake would have observed the huge rock faces rising from the shore, the tributary rivers choked with rapids and the thick forests of spruce, pine, tamarack and birch. On reaching the upper end of the lake, the picture changes, shorelines are gradual and the land flattens out to an expansive triangular plain of arable clay.[21] It is not surprising that those early surveyors came away so impressed with what they saw.

The Temiskaming and, further north, the Cochrane clay belts are both products of the receding Laurentide ice front of some 10,000 years ago. Waters dammed by the northern margin of the ice and a ridge of glacial deposits to the south first formed Lake Barlow-Ojibway. Originally held within the deep trench that is now Lake Temiskaming, the waters eventually broke through and drained down the Ottawa Valley, leaving the two regions to the north spread with thick clays.[22] The deep, level soil was to be an agricultural boon. Around the perimeter of the clay, the rocky outcroppings of the Shield proved to be geologically fertile, yielding large deposits of silver and gold.[23]

The heart of Temiskaming is the 68-mile-long lake whose name means "deep waters." Deep yet sometimes shallow with sandbars, wide yet with pincer-like narrows, it has a natural beauty. The lake's weather can be as changeable as its topography, making its waters a challenge to navigate. Several large rivers feed Temiskaming, draining the watershed south of the Height of Land some fifty miles north of the head of the lake. At the upper end of the lake, the Des Quinze River flows from its source in northern Quebec; the Blanche River and Wabi Creek enter from the north and west; the Montreal, Metabetchouan and Kipawa rivers enter at the

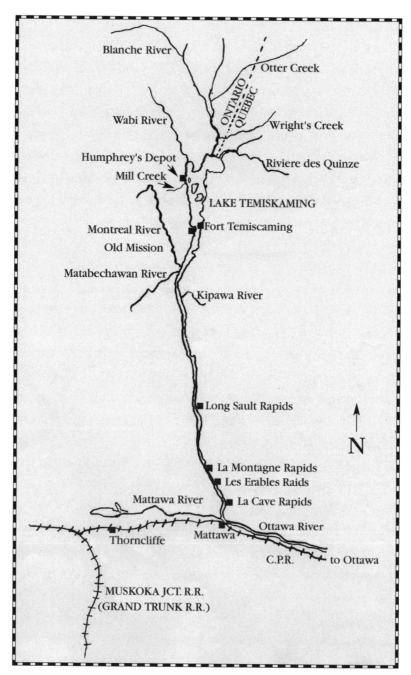

A sketch map of Lake Temiskaming and the Upper Ottawa River.

southern end. As the lake narrows to the south, the Ottawa River is formed. It abruptly descends 53 1/2 feet in a little more than seven miles through the Long Sault, "a formidable rapid," as described in a Government Report of 1895,[24] then into Seven League Lake. For about twenty miles the water is navigable and extremely deep; some soundings have reached 400 feet in depth. In the final fourteen miles to Mattawa, the Ottawa drops another twenty-eight feet through another series of four hazardous rapids before meeting the Mattawa River. The evolution of the Ottawa system is complete, having travelled from river to lake and back to river.

Colonization of the Temiskaming area took place first along the Quebec side. In 1848, Bishop Guigues of Ottawa mandated the Oblate missionaries to evangelize the Native population as far as Hudson Bay. They began their work in earnest and, in 1863, established the mission of St. Claude on the Ontario shore at the narrows opposite Fort Temiskaming. It grew to include a chapel, farm, hospital, school and orphanage run by the Grey Sisters. Meanwhile, settlement was increasing on the Quebec side, spearheaded by Fr. Charles Paradis. Edouard Piche was the first to establish a farm in Guigues Township. Baie-des-Pères, an attractive harbour just north of Fort Temiskaming, became the site of the town of Ville-Marie, named after the patroness of the Oblates; and by 1887 the old St. Claude Mission was moved over to the townsite. It was the success of this thriving community, combined with lessening animal stocks for trapping, that led to the decline of the old Hudson's Bay post. By 1886 the fur trade was transferred to Mattawa House, the Fort itself finally closing down in 1891.[25]

Before the 1880s, settlement along the Ontario shore of Lake Temiskaming was haphazard. Some farmers from the Quebec side came over to grow hay for cattle feed, while some traders, hoping

The flat "Little Clay Belt" farmland at the head of the lake, Dymond Township, on Harley Line, looking west from Highway 11. Courtesy of Lorene DiCorpo.

to make some additional money, "squatted" (without title) on land where they grew hay to sell to the Hudson's Bay Company at Fort Temiskaming. It was this latter enterprise that caught the attention of the then Fort Temiskaming Factor, Charles Cobbold Farr. Interested not only in the produce but the land itself, he worked to purchase and gain legal title of the land around what was then called Humphrey's Depot. With great zeal he promoted the settlement potential of the area, writing letters and pamphlets to the provincial government and to England as well. His diligence paid off. His little village, renamed Haileybury after his old school in England, officially became a post office in 1890.[26] The exploration and survey of the surrounding townships opened up the area to farming, although this was slow to come. The main impetus for population growth came with the discovery of silver just to the south in the Cobalt Lake area. The town of Haileybury became the entry point for the influx of entrepreneurs and speculators that followed, aided in 1905 by the extension of the Temiskaming and Northern Ontario Railway to the adjoining settlement of New Liskeard. Destroyed by fire in 1906, the town was rebuilt. In 1912, again through the persistent promotion and lobbying of its founder, C.C. Farr, Haileybury won the distinction of District Town for Temiskaming. These seemed to be the glory years for the town. Fire destroyed it again in 1922 but it was rebuilt once more. Its fortunes rose and fell with the success and decline of mining ventures, and eventually returned to its agricultural beginnings as an economic base.

SURVEYING FOR SETTLEMENT IN NEW ONTARIO

In the post-Confederation nineteenth century, Canada was still land of "hewers of wood and drawers of water," and settlement was seen as the key to economic growth. The province of Ontario south of the French and Mattawa rivers, known as Upper Canada, had been largely developed by the early waves of pioneers, primarily through agriculture and logging. In some areas free grant townships were offered to lure settlers. As well, the Colonization Roads built to allow access to the townships continued to expand, as did the demand for more good agricultural land. Eastern Upper Canada, south of the Ottawa River, lacked the big expanses of fertile soil found in the southwest. Throughout intensive logging was exhausting the old-growth stands of timber. People who lived off the land needed to look elsewhere for their livelihood.

When, in the 1880s, the Canadian Pacific Railway cut across the northern fringe of Old Ontario[27] and the Grand Trunk system pushed north from Gravenhurst towards Lake Nipissing, roads of steel became the way through the hinterland to the west.

Temiskaming settlers. Courtesy of the Archives of Ontario, C147, from *Temiskaming Views*, 1897.

Ironically, the quick survey of townships along the planned route of the CPR did not reveal the boundless rich soil that would attract farmers.[28] Instead, the accidental discovery of copper and nickel in the Sudbury area initially brought an influx of mining and business speculators. The land was to be exploited in a different way.

The quest for good agricultural land continued. In the early 1880s, Ontario Crown Lands Commissioner, T.B. Pardee, sent Public Lands Surveyor, Alexander Niven, to run exploration and base lines in the area between Lakes Nipissing and Temiskaming. Niven outlined townships to the southwest edge of Lake Temagami, finding more of the typical Shield country of rock, forest and lakes. Around the same time the Quebec government, at the urging of French-Canadian Oblate missionaries, was carrying on a settlement project up the eastern side of Lake Temiskaming into a fertile clay belt.[29]

In 1885, Niven was sent back to the Temiskaming area to

continue exploration and run township base lines. This time he found evidence not only of rock and forest but of the same tracts of clay soil as on the Quebec side, stretching beyond the northern edge of the lake. His favourable report to the Crown Lands Department was the go-ahead for the subsequent twenty years of intense exploration and survey carried out in the north, ultimately opening it up to development of both its agricultural and mineral wealth.

EARLY SURVEYING PRACTICES IN ONTARIO

About two miles west of Cochrane an historic plaque recalls an event significant to the province's past and present. It marks the point where the meridian line, run over 100 years ago by Ontario Land Surveyor Alexander Niven, crosses Highway 11 on its route from the Algoma-Sudbury boundary to the shores of James Bay. Symbolically it is commemorative of all the early surveyors who contributed to the development of Northern Ontario. Without the advance work of the surveyor, settlers could not have fulfilled the dream of owning their own piece of land. Unfortunately, there is little public awareness of the efforts of the land surveyors who first explored, outlined and surveyed the townships and planned the townsites. The enduring monuments to these men are evident in their work, the roads that were built along the township lines they ran; the orderly plan of towns and the institution of laws that maintain the original lines as the standard for assessing property boundaries.

The first surveys in Canada under the direction of civil authority were made when the British formally acquired the land in 1763. However, it would be over 75 years later before an act was

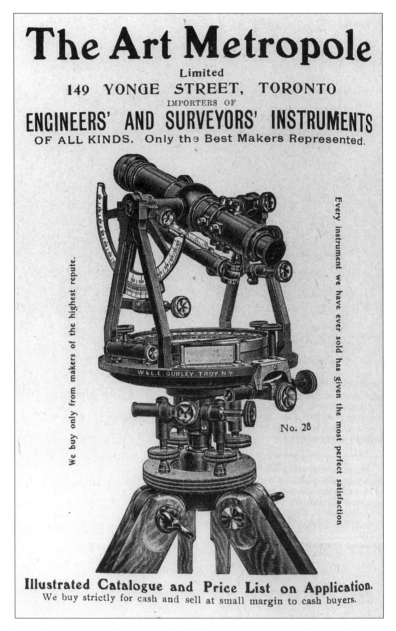

An advertisement for an early 20th-century surveyor's transit.

Courtesy of the Archives of Ontario. Lib. Period. Association of Ontario Land Surveyors Annual Report, 1909.

The canoe was an essential mode of transportation and exploration for the surveyor. Courtesy of the Haliburton Highlands Museum.

passed regulating the profession of land surveying and setting standards for education, training and practice of the surveyors. The minimum age for applicants was twenty-one. Subjects for examination included a variety of maths and technical skills: geometry, trigonometry, measurement, mapping and astronomy. An apprenticeship of three years under a qualified surveyor completed the rigorous training. In 1886, surveyors in Ontario organized as the Association of Provincial Land Surveyors and, in 1892, were incorporated as the Association of Ontario Land Surveyors.[30]

For the surveys completed in the late 1800s, north of the French and Mattawa rivers, the model established in the United States – a six-mile square township – was followed. The vast, rugged country where logging and mining prevailed made the former 1,000 and 2,400 acre sectional system unsuitable. The large townships they produced were an unwieldy size to administer.

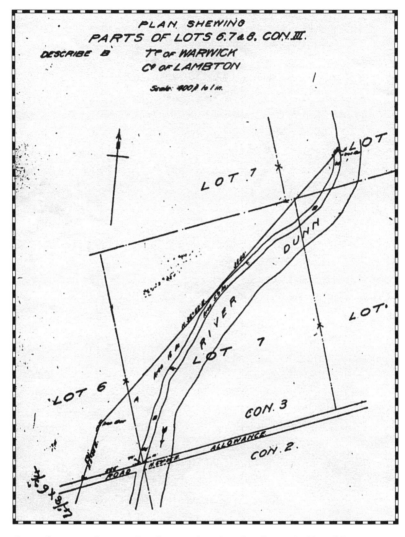

Sample pages from a final examination for Ontario Land Surveyor certification. Courtesy Archives of Ontario. Lib. Period. Association of Ontario Land Surveyors Final Examination, February 1911.

By 1906, the economic advantage of administering a larger township, among other reasons, resulted in another change, this time to a 9-mile square township. However, these larger divisions

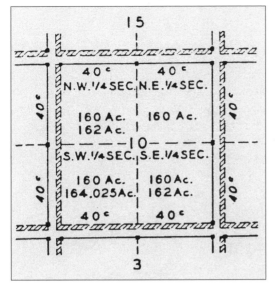

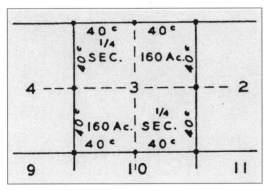

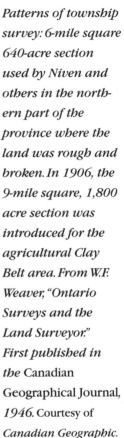

Patterns of township survey: 6-mile square 640-acre section used by Niven and others in the northern part of the province where the land was rough and broken. In 1906, the 9-mile square, 1,800 acre section was introduced for the agricultural Clay Belt area. From W.F. Weaver, "Ontario Surveys and the Land Surveyor." First published in the Canadian Geographical Journal, 1946. Courtesy of Canadian Geographic.

continued to follow the north-south, east-west orientation of the 6-mile square.

All of these surveys were cadastral,[31] they delineated boundaries and property lines. All were done in those times with instruments that were primitive by today's standards and without the benefit of aerial mapping. Compasses and link chains were typical equipment. Astronomical readings were performed using the North Star (Polaris) as reference point to complete maps of the

Historical plaque commemorating Niven's Meridian, near Cochrane, Ontario. Courtesy of Chris Oslund, Curator, Haileybury Heritage Museum.

survey. Until 1903, lot corners were marked with wooden posts, subject to the ravages of weather and forest fires. Despite limitations, these surveys have withstood the test of time. Original maps, drawings and field notes[32] are still available for reference at the Survey Records branch of the Ministry of Natural Resources. Niven's Meridian, which he ran in 1898, was and continues to be a benchmark survey line in the north.

THE SURVEY TRIP – 1886

Assistant Crown Lands Commissioner Aubrey White. Niven was under government contract and answered directly to White, providing him with reports and financial accounts. Courtesy of the Archives of Ontario, Lib. Period. Association of Ontario Land Surveyors Annual Report, 1908.

On May 29, 1886, Assistant Crown Lands Commissioner Aubrey White summoned Alexander Niven to Toronto to discuss the completion of the job begun the year before: the survey of the seven townships at the head of Lake Temiskaming. Niven began preparations from his Haliburton home, hiring as crew local brothers James and Joseph Heard, Robert Andrews and four men whom he wired at Mattawa. Robert Andrews was a long-time resident of Haliburton and owner of a general store. James Hurd and his younger brother Joseph (who preferred the spelling Heard) were experienced bushmen and local contractors with connections to English aristocracy.

Shortly after, Alexander Herkes Telfer, Thomas H. Botham of York Mills, and Hugh R. Baines, a civil engineer with offices on Richmond Street in Toronto, all of the Toronto area, signed on. They travelled the Ontario and Quebec line of the CPR to meet Niven's party at Peterborough. Finally, C.F. Aylsworth, a recently accredited surveyor from Madoc, joined them at Ivanhoe Station in Huntington township, Hastings County, on a new line running northeast adjacent to the Belleville and North Hastings Railway.[33]

Expenses, including salaries, equipment and supplies for at least three months, were strictly accounted for. A trip of this kind would hold Niven indebted to a typical sum of $2,000 to $2,500. At a time when a labourer's daily wages were measured in amounts of a dollar or less, this was a considerable financial undertaking. For men like A.H. Telfer, with a family to support, it was a promise of employment in an exciting environment of yet-to-be charted territory. Like their forebears who braved the voyage to the new world, few, including himself, were fully aware of the dangers and backbreaking tasks ahead. The following is A.H. Telfer's personal account of his experiences as a member of the Temiskaming survey crew.

PART TWO

Diary of
A.H. Telfer – 1886

Diary of A.H. Telfer – 1886

Notes of a trip from Toronto to Lake Temiscamingue and back
In company with Mr. A. Nevin, P.L.S.

For the purpose of running township boundaries on the
west shore near the head of the lake

York Mills P.O., Ontario

Year - 1886

July 19th:

Left Toronto at 10:30 am by the CPR.[1] Passed through a fine country for the first 20 miles. It then became stony and rough as far as Perth, [the rail line was from Peterborough, towards Perth and eventually Carleton] a town of considerable size, but very scattering; below that point, very rocky, worse than Muskoka, but better towards Peterborough;[2] quite a large town, compact, the country flat and swampy, flat rocks with a covering of soil. Arrived at Carleton Jct. [today Carleton Place] about 6 pm, and waited till 1 am next morning for a train to take us to Mattawa, on the main line of the CPR.

First railway station at Mattawa, built in 1881 by the CPR. It was later destroyed by fire. The present building on site was erected in 1902. Courtesy of the Canadian Pacific Archives, A.17135.

July 20th:

Mattawa is a nice little town with some fine stone buildings, built of the stones found in the neighbourhood, in layers of a bluish slate colour, having a very pleasing appearance.[3] Arrived here at 9 am, had dinner at 10, and then commenced looking up supplies. Mr. Nevin procured one large, strong boat and three birch bark canoes. Hired three Frenchmen and one Indian,[4] and then we proceeded to load our stuff in the boat.

Viz. 20 bags of flour

1600 lb. pork

150 H. beans

100 H. sugar

50 H salt

1 chest of tea

half a bushel split peas

1 barrel dried apples

1 keg syrup

a quantity of soap

a few pounds of rosin, for mending birch bark canoes

axes and handles

1 grindstone

1 brush hook

gun and rifle

cooking utensils

590 lbs. Sea biscuits

surveyors instruments

1 bag full of clothes, shoes for each man – 12 men in all. So that with men, supplies, baggage and instruments, our frail craft were well loaded, having also 4 tents.

We left Mattawa about 5 pm, and got 4 miles up the river and camped for the night.

Sketch of Hudson Bay Fort, Mattawa, 1884-1886. Courtesy of the Archives of Ontario, C273-1-0-49-40.

Ottawa River below site of Long Sault Rapids. Courtesy of Lorene DiCorpo.

July 21st:

Started up the river, which is about a quarter of a mile wide, with steep banks from 250 to 300 ft. high, covered with Norway pine, spruce and cedar, forming a lovely border to this beautiful river; and it is surprising to see those pines from 8 to 12 inches through, clinging to the bare rock in many places where scarcely an inch of soil is to be seen. The Ottawa would be a most magnificent public highway were it not for the many rapids, which seem to break the navigation.[5] When we get to these rapids, if they are bad ones, we have to land, unload all our stuff and carry it past the rapids, then carry the canoes. In other places, a rope is fastened to the bow of the canoe, and from 3 to 5 men pull on the rope on shore, while one or two wade by the side of the boat and keep it out of the rocks and boulders, till the rapid is passed. At other times, all hands have to plunge into the water to their waist and pull on the ropes, stumbling over the large, slippery stones, where it would be almost impossible to stand without the rope; by that means, each man helps to hold up his companion.

Made 6 miles today.

July 22nd:

Commenced the assent of Seven League Lake this morning. This is simply a widening of the river with no swift currents for 21 miles. Fine scenery on the riverbanks, and pleasant paddling.

July 23rd:

Today we encountered the Six Mile Rappids[6] where we had plenty of hard work. It is not one continuous rappid, but the few intervening stretches of navigable water are short, however. Mr. Nevin [led], but a team and took us to the commencement of Lake Temiscamingue about 4 pm. The bark canoes were carried over the road; the last mile of that road beat all I ever saw – a waggon load drawn over large boulders, and so close together that the wheels rarely touched the ground. The Frenchmen took the large boat up the rappids; we then loaded up again. Just then, a steamboat came in sight with a raft of square timber in tow.[7] Mr.

The steamship Argo *hauled a variety of cargo and passengers up and down Lake Temiskaming, while towing rafts of timber.* Courtesy of the Archives of Ontario, Jones Collection, C147-1-0-1-2 (AO 4588).

Engine room of the Argo. It provided a warmer place than the open deck for A.H. Telfer to bed down for the night. Courtesy of the Archives of Ontario, Jones Collection, C147-1-0-2-15 (AO 4591).

Nevin said he would see if he could make the steamer, which had by this time cut loose from the raft and laid up at the wharf. We then started, paddled past the steamer up to the raft and stopped there to wait for Mr. Nevin. After waiting for some time, between hope and fear he told us to go back to the steamer and put our stuff on board. This was welcome orders, and obeyed with alacrity. Our stuff all on board, and the canoes too, the large boat towed behind, we then started northward, having nothing to do but promenade the deck and enjoy the beautiful scenery of Lake Temiscamingue.

The Narrows, looking north. The old Catholic Mission is on the left; Fort Temiskaming is on the Quebec side. Courtesy of the Archives of Ontario, Jones Collection, C147-3-0-3-2.

HBC *Fort Temiskaming. C.C. Farr was factor there in 1886, but was already staking out a homestead at Humphrey's Depot. He was soon to resign his post to engage full-time in promoting settlement, and to found the town of Haileybury.* Courtesy of the Archives of Ontario, Jones Collection, C147-1-0-1-4 (AO4589).

Some were drying wet shirts, socks and blankets while the sun shone. After dark, all hands sought some place to lie down to sleep; some on deck, some under the canoes, and some down in the hold beside the stoker. I commenced on deck, and finished near the engine where it was warm, and slept as well as could be expected under the circumstances, waking the next morning when the sun was shining bright in Fort Temiscamingue.

July 24th:

The Fort proper, or Hudson's Bay Trading Post, is on the Quebec side. There are 4 or 5 large buildings, some very old; I noticed the date 1811 painted on one.[8] There are several others, all occupied by Indians.[9] I saw only three white men there. Lots

Some inhabitants of the Fort community. Courtesy of the Archives of Ontario, Jones Collection, C147-1-0-1-8 (AO 4590).

of little fat papooses waddling and tumbling around. About a dozen small tents were pitched around the fort on the beach, all occupied by Indians. The squaws,[10] young and old, were peeping out of the tent doors, taking stock of us as we went into the storehouse to get some things required by the men. I bought a cap – $1.00, 1 pair of wool mits – $.50. Some bought blankets, 8 and 10 dollars per pair, sashes, tobacco and matches. On the west, or Ontario side is the Roman Catholic Mission Station, consisting of a church, the priest's residence and out buildings, and 3 or 4 neat log houses occupied by Indians. The priest has a very nice garden, in which he has plenty of red currants, beans ready to use, tomatoes in bloom and tobacco 18 inches high.

We left the fort about 10 am and started northward of the lake, leaving Mr. Nevin and the Indian Petri to follow on Sunday.

Arrived at our camping ground at 4 pm, went ashore and unloaded everything. We pitched four tents; one for the provisions, one for the cook, two for sleeping in. It was raining at the time, making it very disagreeable. We camped at the mouth of a small creek on which there is a gristmill and sawmill owned by John Piche, whose friends live on the Quebec side. These mills are of the most primitive description, but answer the purpose very well. I saw some of flour in the gristmill. The proprietor, Mr. [Edouard] Piche, was very much disappointed that Mr. Coster did not come this far; he would have spent two weeks with him to show him the country and board him free, no other settlers [being] here on this side of the lake.[11]

Sunday, July 25th:

First Sunday away from home. Thought much of my loved ones there, and knew they were thinking of me, and wondering where I was. May God protect them and bless them, and grant that we may meet again in safety. We lay around in camp resting. In the afternoon, Baines [his background is mentioned in the section prior to the diary] and I paid a visit to Mr. Piche. Examined his mill and clearing. He has about fifteen acres cleared. His yoke of oxen is composed of a bull and a cow. He is a young man with a wife and two children. They feel rather lonesome here, and no wonder.

July 26th:

Commenced work this morning by going down the Lake to the north boundary of the township surveyed by Mr. Nevin last year, called "Lorraine," [named after Reverend Narcisse Lorrain, Roman Catholic Bishop of Pontiac, Quebec][12] followed the boundary to the north-west corner, then commenced to run north on a line to strike the Lake. Some places very rocky. Crossing a deep creek on a tree Tom Botham [mentioned earlier as being from North York, Ontario] fell in up to the neck.[13]

After passing over a high rocky ridge, we struck a piece of low, level land of very good quality, timbered with tamarack, balsam, whitewood and a few pines. Did not reach the lake today.

July 27th:

Commenced where we left off last night, and ran north to the lake; struck a clearing belonging to Hudson Bay [Hudson's Bay Company], Mr. [C.C.] Farr,[14] Manager. Passed through good land today. Left the instruments in the field. Hay all still standing. Indians and Frenchmen are poor farmers.

July 28th:

Finished the line out to the lake, and some traverse lines on the beach, then went back to camp to dinner. Had visitors from the Fort. Mr. Farr and family came last night, and had supper, breakfast and dinner with us. After dinner, started again at the northwest corner of Lorraine and ran west – Mr. Nevin, Mr. Baines, French John and I; Jas. and Jos. Heard being off chopping on a place they wish to claim; [When the Crown Lands Department in 1891 released the surveyed townships for sale, Niven purchased a section immediately north of Humphrey's Depot (owned by C.C. Farr); James Heard purchased the remaining northern sections of the lot and all of lot eleven, Concession 4 to the west[15]] the other men tracking and moving camp, returning at night. We found our new campground on the bank of a creek where it is crossed by the old Portage Trail[16] from the head of the lake to the Montreal River. Good land, timber, spruce, tamarack, whitewood, white birch, etc. Sand flies are a terrible pest, worse than mosquitoes by far.

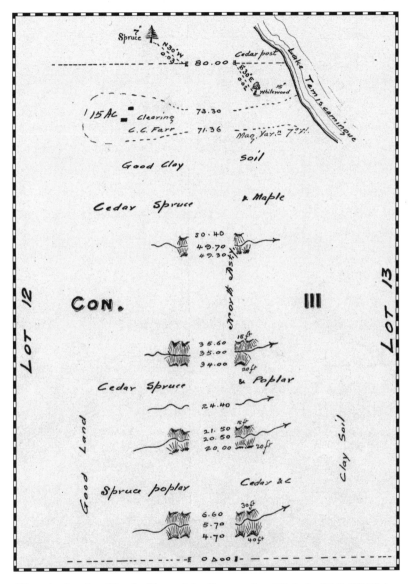

Niven's sketch of Bucke Township, Concession III, Lots 12 & 13. Note the split-line method of relating measurements to topographical features, a simplified recording system begun in 1859. Niven, O.L.S., Field Notes, 1886. Source: Ontario Ministry of Natural Resources. Copyright: 2002, Queen's Printer, Ontario.

July 29th:

Crossed the creek by canoe at the camp and struck through the bush and continued to run westward, crossed over a high, rocky ridge; when on the summit, could see for miles on each side. When coming back to camp, we passed the end of it where it ran out at the creek. There were perpendicular walls of rock more than 100 feet high. We arrived at camp with a large appetite, and found the cook had a good supper of soup, baked beans, pork, apples, twisters [bread dough that, instead of being baked, was boiled in savoury or sweet liquid to suit the occasion] and syrup, which received prompt attention.

July 30th:

Struck camp this morning and every man took a bag on his back and carried over the old trail to the creek, about half a mile. Continued the line westward, and ran a little over a mile; camped again tonight on a nice dry spot on the bank of the creek. Mr. Nevin and Jas. Heard stayed out on the line all night to take an observation. Had blankets and provisions sent to them. It rained a small shower in the evening. They made a tent of their blankets.

July 31st:

Struck camp again this morning. Each man carried his baggage as far as the line was open, and left it for the Frenchmen to bring on, then [we] resumed our work on the line. About noon struck a beautiful lake, in which are lovely little islands covered with spruce. It took considerable time to get around the end, the surveyor having to take an angle. We got nearly half a mile on the west side. The tents and provisions were got over and camp pitched on the west side. I had the misfortune to cut my knee this afternoon.

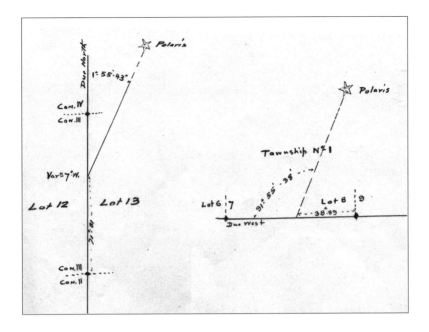

Astronomical observations were essential to the accurate calculation and drawing of township lines. From Niven's Field Notes, 1886, 99. Source: Ontario Ministry of Natural Resources. Copyright: 2002, Queen's Printer, Ontario.

August 1st:

Sunday, a fine day, warm morning. Some of the men went fishing, and caught some perch.

No sound of church bells ever echo over the shores of this little sylvan lake. My thoughts are constantly turning to my loved ones at home. I know they are thinking of me and wondering where I am, and what I am doing. God grant that we may all meet again in health and unbroken family. Had fish for dinner today: Grey trout and perch. We had a thundershower in the afternoon and evening. We turned in early. It is a somewhat novel sensation to be on a brush bed, and listen to the rain pattering on the tent so near to your head.

August 2nd:

My knee feels very stiff this morning.[17] I would like to rest today, but we must strike camp, and everything must be moved. So we start off on the line about 3 o'clock, strike another lake, which we find too long to go around. Our pack men were to meet us at this lake with the canoe to take us across, but failed to find us. French John was sent to look for them, and found them camped about a mile and a half away. About sunset he returned with the canoe. It took two trips to take us, as the canoe would not carry all of us at once.

Land today very stony and rocky. Cedar, balsam, spruce trees.

August 3rd:

Left camp this morning, travelling around the small lake at our camp to the one we struck yesterday; then the canoes took us to the line, and we started west again, and reached the western boundary of the township about 3 o'clock, where we planted a large square corner post; then started northward. This line, when finished, will be 24 miles long. The land today was very poor, having been burnt over at some time.[18] The timber is small and scrubby, the bottom nearly all rock and stones. In a hollow it was completely paved with stones as large as a man could lift, packed close together, like hailstones after a shower. Passed one beaver meadow on the line northward. Poor land today.

August 4th:

Broke camp again this morning and carried out stuff around the end of the lake, the canoe bringing the rest. We intended to leave the stuff, about a mile ahead of where we quit last night, but got half a mile too far west. Very poor land today most of it burnt over and grown up with small brush and berries. Many raspberries are getting ripe. Mr. Baines cut his foot very bad on the inside, near the instep, and had to go back to camp, French John going with him. He will not be able to do anything for some weeks and likely have to be taken out to Lake Temiscamingue. The Boss sleeps on the line tonight to take an observation.

August 5th:

Continued the line north,[19] passed over two high ridges of rock, a kind of reddish brown slate stone all broken up to blocks of every conceivable size, easily hammered or split. Poor land. Even the valleys are full of stones. Lots of huckleberries today.

August 6th:

Struck a branch of Wahbe's Creek today. The Boss gave orders to bring the stuff up by it, in the canoe, but it was so crooked and full of logs that it only proved a hindrance. No improvement on the land yet. If we want a drink and don't find running water we throw out the loose stones and soon find water.

My knee is pretty stiff yet.

August 7th:

Slept on beds made of marsh grass last night. Considerably quite, quite a luxury.

Our pack men have had a hard time for a day or two getting the stuff forward.

Started again northward on the line; the land rose gradually, till we reached a ridge of rock 250 feet high from which we had the most beautiful view I have ever seen.[20] The view extended westward 10 or 12 miles, north and northwest 20 miles, looking over the top of a forrest of spruce, balsam, birch and poplar. One vast sea of undulating green foliage, bounded on the west by hills covered with the dark green of spruce and balsam. On some, the bare rock was plainly visible. Far away to the north, the view was bounded by a blue ridge, stretching away in a northwesterly direction over the vast expanse of green. The course of the small streams could be traced by the darker lines of balsam along their margin. This was a most charming picture worth travelling miles to see. On the north side, this rock declines precipitously, the descent being rather difficult, letting yourself down from one narrow ledge to another, being careful to avoid the loose stones; the rocks in this neighbourhood being all broken up into small blocks and full of seams.

This afternoon, we reached the northwest corner of the township [Bucke], and turned east toward Temiscamingue again.

[*August 8th*[21] *to September 4th - No entries*]

September 4th:

All this time lost, nursing my leg,[21] under the roof of Mr. Edward Piche,[22] an old veteran French Canadian, whose wife was an Irish woman. Very kind people who treated me, a total stranger, with the greatest kindness and solicitation for my comfort and recovery. Their family consists of two daughters, grown up, and a boy of fourteen. They have had a large family, but these are all that are now at home. Two of their daughters are nuns at Ottawa. Yesterday, I was very glad to see our men coming along the shore from the head of the Lake, looking for me.[23] I was sorry Mr. and Mrs. Piche were away at their eastern farm about three miles distant, so I bade the young people goodbye, and started with my old comrades. We went down the eastern shore to the silver mine there.[24] Not much doing at present, except sawing lumber for their buildings. They intend putting up a smelter as soon as they get the machinery all on the ground. The mine is on the shore, close to the water. No great quantity of ore has yet been taken out, but so far has proved rich in silver and lead. We secured several specimens, and started for the west shore, but found the lake so rough, we had to turn back and wait for two hours. We started again, and made out to reach [Piche's] mill where we camped for the night on the same ground where we had camped first on Lake Temiscamingue.

September 5th:

Sunday. Went across West Bay to where the rest of our gang were camped, unloaded our boat, and pitched our tents, then wandered along the shore and round Wahnaby's Point,[25] inspecting the limestone rocks and picking up curious stones on the beach. Wahnaby's farm was deserted and rather desolate looking. This morning, one of the Frenchmen, John Grenion, had words [an argument] about the work, which resulted in his leaving Monday morning.

On leaving Mr. Piche's, they gave me a lot of onions which were very much relished by all the gang.[26]

September 6th:

We started across West Bay to the mouth of Wahnaby's Creek (or Caticumni River). For about 3 or 4 miles it is about 4 rods wide with a stiff current. There is good land on each side of the banks; from 6 to 10 feet high, with good land on both sides, black loam with clay bottom. Timber: balsam, spruce, tamarack, cedar, some elm and a few small oaks. We went up the creek 4 or 5 miles, a very pleasant trip until it grew shallow; we then got out, and struggled to push the boat up for a short distance, but finally had to unload and carry our stuff to the line.

Present-day view of the mouth of Wabi Creek where it enters Lake Temiskaming at New Liskeard. Courtesy of Lorene DiCorpo.

This morning, we left everything we could possibly spare at the Bay in the house of one Tousan, a half-breed,[27] to be brought round the point and up the Blanche River, to meet us where the line crosses. We struck the line near the southern boundary of Township No. 3 [Harley] on the plan of survey, and running north, went through about 2 miles of very flat and wet [land], then to the boundary between 3 and 4. Good land, black loam and clay bottom; timber – cedar, birch, tamarack, spruce and poplar. This occupied the whole week, having to run two miles north on no. 4 and 11/2 m. on boundary between [Townships] 3 and 4.

Sunday, September 12th:
Considerable rain last night, patter, pattering, not on the shingles but on the canvas close to your ear. A few nights ago we had a novel experience in that line. While lying on our brush bed, some sleeping and snoring, others awake, listening to the patter, patter of the rain, the canvas becoming wet and heavy, and our

ridge pole being too light, it bent and slipped out of the post, and down came the whole tent on top of us. Baines, lying on his back and snoring, was nearly strangled, as the water began to come through as soon as the canvas fell. There was considerable sputtering and strong talk for a minute, but the Frenchman jumped up and soon put things to right. Today we are a motley looking group, some lounging in the tents, some mending boots and shoes, some patching pants that have been patched before, so that it would puzzle a lawyer to tell which was the original. Patches of every conceivable shape and colour, and pants of rare shape and style; those reaching to the knee being called High Water Pants; pants sewn with thread, patches sewed with fishing line, patches sewed with boot laces, and holes that defy patching are voted a compleat system of ventilation.

Our cook is baking light bread. This he does by digging a hole in the ground about 3 feet long, two feet wide and two feet deep. He makes a fire in this hole to dry and heat it, having his bread ready in two large round bake pans, which he puts into the hole, putting hot ashes and clay, or what is better, sand, below and over them. It is wonderful how well it will bake, and makes good bread. When he has no time to make it that way, the twisters are made and boiled in pork gravy. They are very light and nice while fresh. These with pork, boiled or fried, beans and stewed apples generally contribute our bill of fare, with sometimes a pot of pea soup by way of variation, not forgetting the never failing accompaniment of strong tea.

September 13th (14, 15):
Started on the line running east between 4 and 5. First mile was good land, then it became stony for about a mile with light, gravelly soil, then swamp for a mile or more, then dryer and better

land being intersected by several small ravine. Reached the corner this evening (15th); take a flying camp, moving it along as we go.

September 16th:

Started this morning to continue the line eastward to the Blanche River, which we reached sooner than expected. It crosses the southwest corner of township no. 5 [Brethour] of the Plan of the Survey. We then ran the line from the corner north to the river, and finished both pieces before 10 o'clock am. Rested awhile, had our dinner, and started back to our camp, where we left our cook, a distance of 6 miles. Each man had some load to carry. We reached camp about 5 o'clock, tired and hungry.

September 17th:

Started again northward, on the western boundary of township no. 4. [Hilliard]. Moving camp up the line and getting to work about 10 o'clock, we made a little over a mile. The land was good, except a quarter of a mile was stony.

September 18th:

Continued the line north today, nearly two miles, land first class, a rich black loam underlaid by a marly friable clay, not like the tough, heavy clay of the southern counties of Ontario. I believe no better soil for general farming can be found in the Dominion.

September 19th Sunday:

A wet, drizzly, disagreeable day. I got up before anyone else in camp. Did not sleep much, being crowded too much in bed. Don't like Mr. Baines for a bedfellow, he is the most persistent and inveterate snorer I have ever encountered.

It stopped raining about 5 o'clock pm. The first frost of the season we had on the evening of the 12th. On the 15th, it froze ice in the water in our pails. This is considered early in this part of the country but as everything is ripe, it will do little or no harm.

September 20th:

Continued the western boundary northward, and reached the corner about 5 o'clock pm, this being our farthest northern limit. We have now followed this line 24 miles from our southernmost starting point. We will next strike east until we come to the Blanche River. The ground we have passed over today was mostly cedar swamp; at the corner, tamarack and spruce. Soil good, no stones.

September 21st:

Continued the line running east, being the northern boundary of our six townships. The cedar swamp continued all day,

The Blanche River, near present-day Englehart. Courtesy of Lorene DiCorpo.

very bad travelling. Had to camp in a beastly place tonight. Very bright starlight when we went to bed, but woke up to find it raining before daylight. The worst camping ground we have had yet. There was a large root located under my ribs, and that, mixed with loud snoring, made it anything but a paradise!

September 22nd:

Continued our line east till we struck the River Blanche at 3 o'clock in the afternoon. We got out of the cedar swamp into dryer ground. Spruce and tamarack timber, soil black loam with greyish clay bottom mixed with sand. We expect Tousan to meet us here with the canoe, bringing the rest of our baggage and our mail;[28] however, if he should pass up the river before we reach it with the line, it would be difficult for him to tell where to stop, as we are over 20 miles from the mouth of the river [the Blanche River].

September 23rd:

We heard a shot fired this morning just after breakfast, and made sure it was our man Tousan; and as we were ready to start out to work, we went down to the river, about 15 chains[29] from the camp. On arrival we found not our man Tousan, but two men from the head of the lake, John Simpson, a half-breed, and John Baptiste, an old Indian who was working at Piche's mill when we first arrived. They were up the river on a hunting excursion with apparent indifferent success. We got them to take us across the river in their canoe, leaving the two Frenchmen on the west bank to make a raft to ferry to and from camp till the arrival of Tousan. Mr. Nevin invited the hunters to breakfast, an invitation, which was readily accepted. It was amusing to contemplate the length and breadth and depth of the smile that overspread the countenance of the old Indian. The prospect of a good square meal of pork, beans, bread and tea, it looked like the breaking up of a hard winter.

The river at this point is 10 rod wide at low water, and eleven feet deep. We continued our line eastward, and on getting a few chains away from the river, we came to a large brulie, apparently severall miles in extent; this tract has been burnt over probably 12 or 15 years ago, and the timber wholly consumed. It is now covered with a dense undergrowth of balsam and spruce through which we had to hew our way; the line looking like a ditch 4 or 5 feet wide, 12 or 15 feet deep, and miles in length.

September 24th:

We crossed a good-sized creek this forenoon, and another one in the afternoon, crossing its winding course two or three times. We brought a tent and provisions with us today, to stay overnight and reach the centre line tomorrow. Every appearance of rain tonight. After supper we turned in pretty early. A lively discussion took place on the Scott Act,[30] Mr. Aylsworth taking the anti-Scot, and Mr. Baines the temperance side.

Our man Tousan arrived this morning, or rather last night, but we did not find him untill the morning. He brought our boat and one canoe. It appears that the Frenchman John Gagnon and the Indian Perio, who left us two weeks ago, have each taken a canoe that belonged to Mr. Nevin, leaving us only half our fleet. What gladdened the heart of every man was a large bundle of papers and letters, and although everyone had been wishing for papers for the last two weeks, to see what was going on in the outside world, it was amusing to see how these same papers were tossed aside as of no consequence, until the letters from the loved ones at home are read and re-read.[31] This time, I got two letters from my own loved ones with the welcome news that all were well. This made my heart glad, and rough work seemed lighter than before.

For the past two days, we have been running through the same brulie, thickly covered with small spruce and tamarack. Soil is good.

September 25th:

Raining this morning and forenoon, did not go till after dinner. We then went and finished the line to the corner of the township at the centre line, the corner stake being planted about halfway up a considerable hill. We then returned to our tent, picked up everything and walked back to the main camp at the river; arrived there about sunset, wet, tired and hungry, and did ample justice to the good supper waiting for us. The weather cleared off tonight, and the stars shone bright.

September 26th Sunday:

Raining again this morning. I believe we have not had a dry Sunday since arrival at Temiscamingue. After breakfast, Mr. Nevin and Jas. and Joe Heard started for a trip up the river. I got up early, and washed my shirts, and had my washing out before breakfast. Then, all hands had shirts, pants and socks to mend and dry, moccasins and boots to sew up and repair. In some cases, pants worn badly around the bottom were reduced to High-water order. Tousan brought us a bag of potatoes, a welcome addition to our larder.

The party who went up the river returned about sundown and reported that about 6 miles up or about 23 or 25 miles from the mouth, there is a fall of about four feet.

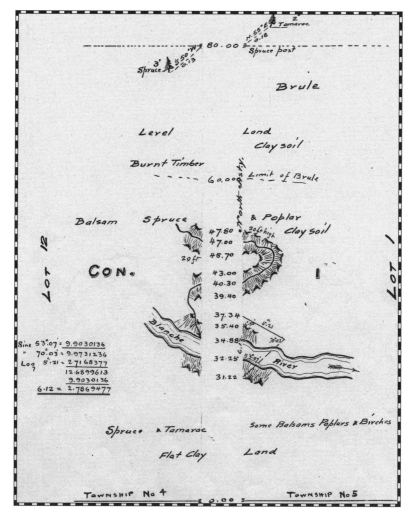

*Niven's sketch of the boundary line between the Townships of
Hilliard (4) and Brethour (5).* From Niven, Field Notes, 1886, 16. Source:
Ontario Ministry of Natural Resources. Copyright: 2002, Queen's Printer,
Ontario.

September 27th Monday:

This morning, we struck camp on the northern boundary and
got everything on board the boat and bark canoe, and moved

down the river to where it crosses the southwest corner of township no. 5, and there pitched our tents again; commenced on the centre line and ran north until night. Found good land here; the timber is birch, spruce, tamarack and poplar, and some cedar.

September 28th:

This morning we took the boat, and went down to the river to where it crosses the line between townships 5 and 6 [Brethour and Casey]. This line has been run from the western boundary to the west bank of the river. We commenced on the east bank, and ran eastward toward the province line [between Quebec and Ontario]. We found good land, a little rolling timber, birch, spruce, tamarack, balsam and cedar.

Near evening, we struck a large creek which we could not cross, and spent some time felling trees into it, but could find none large enough to reach across, so we gave it up and returned to camp.

September 29th:

There have been terrible foreboding and much anxiety in camp for the last few days among the smokers, six in number, as the supply of tobacco was rapidly running out. Many and dire were the threats made by those whose stock was nearly gone, of stealing from those who had a little more, or going on the warpath and turning Tobacco Freebooters. One thing was evident, if tobacco was not forthcoming, the work would stop; for several declared they could not, and would not work without it. So, this morning, Mr. Nevin requested me to take the boat and go down to the lake to J. Piche's, to our storehouse, and bring the tobacco, salt and soap, and go round Wahnby's Point to Tousan's and get him to go across to the storehouse with me. We started

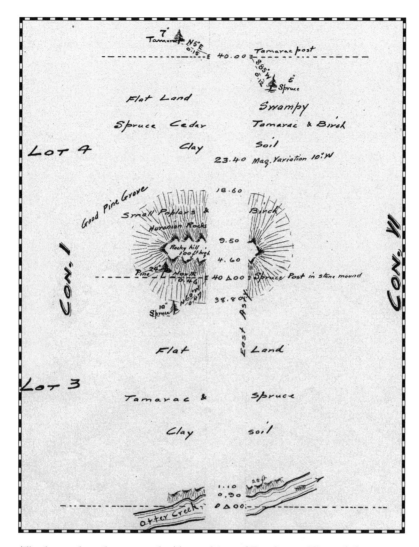

The boundary between the Townships of Brethour (5) and Casey (6). From Niven Field Notes, 80. Source: Ontario Ministry of Natural Resources. Copyright: 2002, Queen's Printer, Ontario.

for camp this morning, all hands taking one tent and everything necessary for a flying camp, as they intended to finish the line east to the province line before coming back. We took the boat, and went down to the mouth of the creek[32] that stopped our progress yesterday. We then went up the creek to the line. The men then took their baggage and provisions ashore, and I turned back on my voyage down to Temiscamingue. The boat is rather large and heavy for one person, and I not being a very expert oarsman, the journey did not partake much of the nature of a picnic; however, the current being in my favour, I got along pretty well untill I reached the lake about four miles up the river. I met a half-breed with his bark canoe, gun, blankets, provisions and a little dog, going up the river to hunt and trap. He expressed compassion for me to man such a big boat, and told me it was 4 miles to the lake, holding up four fingers to make his intelligence more plain. When I got down to the lake, I found a strong wind blowing from the southwest, being right against me, and the water very rough. I had very hard pulling, the wind growing stronger all the while.

I was barely able to reach the southeast corner of Wahnaby's Point, but could not make another foot, so I ran in on the beach and moored the boat to a large stone. On the east side of this point are very high cliffs of white limestone that can be seen for miles. They occur on the south side, but not as high. After moving my boat, I took my provisions, blankets, and axe, and started to walk round the point to Tousan's, it being now near sunset and bad walking over the stones. As I was passing Wahnaby's old house, I was hailed by someone on the bank. On going up, I found it was Tousan, who had come there for a bag of flour he had left there some time previously, so I went with him by a path which cuts across the bush to his house on the west side of the point. He has a neat little log house, an Indian wife, and three small children. Unfortunately, his wife is subject to fits of insanity.

September 30th:

Tousan and I got up early, had breakfast, and dug a bag of potatoes to take back with me; and such potatoes as are seldom seen near Toronto. We then took his bark canoe, and started across west bay, he rowing and I steering, the wind blowing from the same quarter; however, the light canoe was more easily handled than the heavy boat, and we soon arrived at the Mill, found Mr. Piche building a boat, got the key of the storehouse, and secured the much needed tobacco and other articles. Rigging up my blankets for a sail, we scudded back west again at a lively pace, without any work at the oars. We landed where I had left the boat. We transferred everything from the canoe to the boat, including the sail. I bade Tousan goodbye, and started on my voyage back to camp, alone feeling rather uncertain about finding the mouth of the river, as there are a number of sandbars, and much shallow water caused by deposit of matter brought down the river.

I got allong all right, the wind being in my favour untill I came near the mouth of the river, was driven onto the sandbars, and had to take down my sail, push the boat into deeper water, and look for the river, which after considerable time I found more to westward, as will be seen by consulting maps or plans of this region. The Blanche River empties into the lake by two separate mouths or channels. I followed the western on this occasion. I hoped, that after fairly getting into the river, I still would be able to take advantage of the wind, but on hoisting my sail again, found that the wind had gone down, or only came in fitful gusts, doing me more harm than good; so I had to abandon the sail, and rely on my muscle to make the voyage against the current, all the way back to the camp, a distance of nearly fourteen miles. However, night overtook me four miles from the end of my journey. I then went ashore, and made preparation for my stay till morning by lighting a fire, and making a bed of balsam brush. I then ate a hearty supper of bread, pork and river water. Procuring a supply of fuel, I wrapped myself in my blanket, and covered by a rubber raincoat, slept quite comfortably under a large spruce tree, having no one to keep me awake by high pressure snoring, or rob me of one of my blankets by their somnambulistic monopoly of these usefull articles.

Awoke early this morning, and after a sumptuous breakfast of river water, pork and bread, resumed the task of pulling hard against the stream, which, by the way, seems to have been my lot through life.

I arrived at camp between 8 and 9 o'clock, glad once more to see the genial face of our respected cook, who was the sole occupant of the camp at that time.

Shortly after my arrival, it commenced raining and continued about an hour, then turned to snow, which fell heavily untill about five o'clock pm. About 10:30 [am], one of the men came in from the line to assist me in taking the boat back down the river and up the creek to the line and cut out obstructions in the creek, having to cut logs in the water; and it was snowing hard all the time. We were both wet and cold, and concluded to go ashore at the line, and await the arrival of the men. We made a fire, and warmed and dried ourselves as well as we could. Between 5 and 6 o'clock, Mr. Nevin and three of the men arrived, cold and wet, leaving Mr. Aylsworth and J. Sophy to finish the line out to the boundary. As they had a tent with them, Mr. Baines chose to remain all night and come the next morning. After the men had warmed themselves, we started for camp, and as we now manned four oars and a paddle, we went down the creek to the river at a good speed, then up the river to camp.

October 1st:

A very drearily looking morning for the first of October – 3 inches of snow, the trees and boughs bent with the weight.

We struck camp, moved down the river and up the creek,[33] and camped near the centre line running north. We started to work on the line, a most disagreeable task, the snow falling in showers at every stroke. It was three inches deep; it melted on our clothes, ran down our backs and into our boots. When we arrived at camp at night, we were all wet, tired and hungry. After supper, the fire was surrounded by small rods with wet pants, shirts and socks.

October 2nd:

This morning on the line again running north between townships 4 and 5, Aylsworth and Sophy having returned last night. The land on the line running east between 5 and 6 is mostly swampy and wet, except where crossed by one rocky hill 3 1/2 miles from the boundary of the creek. Today, the snow was not so bad, so we only got our feet wet – The land on this line is patches of Brulie, and patches of timber, mostly spruce and tamarack, with some cedar. The Brulies are thickly covered with young spruce and tamarack up to 8 ft. high.

October 3rd Sunday:

A fine day, with high wind taking off the snow and drying the ground, and is being taken advantage of to dry our blankets and clothes. Some patching and mending going on as usual.[34]

The soil in this neighbourhood is black muck or loam, with clay bottom, and although apparently wet at present, would, I think, if cleared, dry up rappidly with the assistance of a few drains.

If it continues fair all day, it will be the first Sunday since coming to Temiscamingue. Oh how I long to see my loved ones at home.

Took a bath – today.

October 4th:

Started again this morning on our line running north between [Townships] 4 and 5. Found a good deal of swamp, rather wet, untill we struck the creek again, 4 1/2 miles from the western boundary. We felled trees into the water to make a bridge. One of the men going down the stream some distance found a crossing, then came up on the opposite bank and felled a large spruce to compleat our bridge.

Our tent was pitched for the night on the east side, water and dry ground being two desirable points in a camping ground. The land is generally dry near the streams. Ran over half a mile on the east side of the creek – .

October 5th:

After gaining the top of the hill, 2 or 3 chains from the corner, the land is slightly rolling, dry and rather lighter soil. Timber, spruce, tamarack, balsam and poplar. It was a hard frost last night. Water brought into the camp early this morning, froze in our tin cups in a few minutes; however, we generally have our tea boiling hot.

The weather has been fine, a few blackflies still remain, but they are by no means so expert in the science of bloodletting as they were a month ago, something to be thankfull for, at least.[35]

October 6th:

Not much frost this morning.

As we had not enough provisions to last untill we finished the line to the province boundary, and go back to camp, Mr. Nevin requested me to go back to camp and bring a further supply, which I did, the distance being four miles to go, and six miles returning. Arrived at camp about 10 o'clock am and found our cook happily blooming alone. Got a supply of bread twisters, and pork, weighing about sixty pounds, and started back to join my comrades, arriving at about 5 o'clock pm, very tired, wet feet, and shirt wet through with perspiration.

October 7th:

About a mile from the corner is nice land, slightly rolling, but yesterday afternoon and this forenoon we came to hills and gullies that made it very bad running, as we have a great deal of chopping that is not required on level land. We crossed the creek twice; the quality of the soil is first class, a black loam on the surface, and a rich clay sub-soil. We are striving to reach the Quebec boundary by Friday night (that is tomorrow).

Hills and ravines all day, which makes it bad surveying, and bad travelling. It is a pity it is not more level, as it is the best soil I ever saw anywhere. We begin to be afraid we will not be able to finish tomorrow.

October 8th:

We got up early this morning, and started out determined to finish today if possible, and luckily we had better running and more level land, so that we reached the Quebec boundary about 4 o'clock pm, striking it 26 chains north of the 13 mile stone,[36] or a little over 13 1/4 miles north of the lake. This boundary line was run about sixteen years ago, and was cut out 20 feet wide, looking like a canal cut through the dense forrest in a straight line, a perpendicular wall of foliage on each side. It is now grown up with thick undergrowth of young tamarack, spruce and balsam. We cut a track through the young undergrowth to the mile stone for our chain men, who chained down to the stone, and found it 26 chains and some links. I understand there is some discrepancy between our measurement and that of the boundary line.[37]

We were all very glad to reach this line today, as it compleats the survey, and leaves us tomorrow to get back to our camp, and rest on Sunday, before starting on the homeward journey.

We compleated our work, planted a post, and returned to our fly camp to rest for the night, having accomplished rather more than we expected in the morning.

October 9th:

We packed up our flying camp this morning, each man taking his load averaging about 50 lbs., and started for the main camp, a distance of over nine miles, having to retrace all the hills and ravines we passed during the last three days - .

Aylsworth, Baines, and the two Frenchmen started off at a fast pace. Mr. Nevin, Jos and Jas. Heard, Thos. Botham and myself took it more leisurely, resting when we got tired and stopped and took dinner at the creek, about three miles from the camp.

Botham, by this time, was beginning to be pretty well played out. We rested an hour and started again. After going half a mile, we discovered that Botham had gone down; so Jos. Heard went back and took his pack and carried it with his own. We then divided some other articles amongst us to make it more equal, and then, proceeded slowly, as it was all he could do to get allong. We arrived at camp about an hour before sundown, very tired, and glad the tramp was over; and ready for the good supper our worthy cook had waiting for us; and happy to think that our tramping and packing was over, and we could quietly rest till Monday morning, and then start for home by boat and canoe.

October 10th Sunday:

We had a few light showers during the night, but a lovely morning dawned and the sun rose bright and clear. We have a warm pleasant day. The whole of the past week has been very fine, and all the traces of our snowstorm compleately vanished. I think that snow storm was an unusual thing in this country, as it is as warm today as it was a month ago.

I wish I could tellegraph to my pets at home that the job is finished, and we start for home tomorrow. It would be joyfull news in that humble cottage!

Very warm all day.

October 11th:

We were all up around half-past four and had breakfast before daylight. Everything is packed up ready to start; by daylight, got down the river, and with the exception of running aground a few times, owing to the creek being so shallow, we reached the beautifull Blanche River. There was more trouble for want of water; the weather was dull and threatening. Evidently, the fine weather of last week is over for the present. We reached the lake safely, and rounded Wanaby's Point, reaching TOUSAN'S farm at 12:30; kindled a fire, and had our dinner; settled some little matter with him, got another bushel of his splendid potatoes. We then bid him goodbye, and proceeded across the bay to John Piche's, took on board the remainder of our stores left there, and then started for Fort Temiscamingue – which, however, we could not reach before dark; so we went ashore in Martin's Bay and camped the night. Very tired, and ready for a rest, having rowed thirty miles or more. The River Blanche is a beautifull highway to travel by boat or canoe, and navigable for steamers of considerable size for at least twenty-five miles, at which point there is a fall of 3 or 4 feet, and even that might be navigable, except at low water.

October 12th:

A damp, chilly morning, got up about seven, and had breakfast, then started again for the fort. After rowing for about an hour, it commenced to rain. The lake was pretty rough and it rained incessantly till we reached the fort. Mr. Farr, the gentleman in charge, kindly placed at our disposal a vacant house, and as it contained an open fire place for which he gave us plenty of wood, we were quite comfortable, after drying ourselves and changing our clothes.

Fort Temiskaming storehouse. Although there seems to be a deliberate arrangement of goods for the photo, the store would have been well-organized. A well-kept garden was part of the compound.
Courtesy of the Archives of Ontario, C147-4-0-6-1.

The Argo *with pointer in tow. The small boat, pointed at both ends, was useful for manoeuvering during logging drives and for transferring passengers and goods to shore in shallow waters.* Courtesy of the Archives of Ontario, Jones Collection, C147-1-0-2-4 (AO 4592).

Mr. Nevin, having decided to go from here by the steamer[38] to the foot of the lake, and from there to Mattawa by the Quebec Colonization Society Line,[39] we stored away here on our boat everything he did not wish to take home with him. This was an arrangement very satisfactory to us under the circumstances. The steamer arrived at the Fort at dusk; we put our stuff on board, and started down the lake. I would rather have gone by daylight, so as to have a better view of the scenery, which is beautiful. The rocks on the shores are in many places very high and steep, varying from 100 to 300 feet.

I got no sleep untill we arrived at the end of the lake on head of the Long Sault. We then went to sleep down in the hold where it was warm, and we rose at 7 in the morning.

October 13th:

Got our breakfast on board, then unloaded our stuff, and put it on the new narrow-gauge railway built by the Temiscamingue Colonisation Society of Quebec, which took us to the foot of the Long Sault, where a small steamer awaited us, and took us eighteen

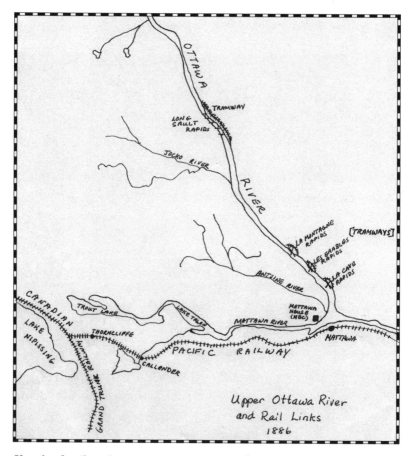

OTTAWA
TRAMWAY
LONG
SAULT
RAPIDS
JOCKO RIVER
RIVER
LA MONTAGNE
RAPIDS
[TRAMWAYS]
LES ERABLES
RAPIDS
LA CAVE
RAPIDS
ANTOINE RIVER
CANADIAN
TROUT LAKE
LAKE TALON
MATTAWA
HOUSE
(HBC)
MATTAWA RIVER
MATTAWA
LAKE
NIPISSING
THORNCLIFFE
PACIFIC   RAILWAY
GRAND TRUNK RAILWAY
CALLENDER

Upper Ottawa River
and Rail Links
1886

Sketch of rail and tram connections, 1886. Courtesy of Lorene DiCorpo.

miles; then a one-horse tramway, then steamer, then tramway, then steamer to Mattawa, where we arrived at 7:30. The rest of the gang took a hurried supper, and went east by train. As I intended to go by Callendar, I stayed all night, thinking to get a train in the morning.

October 14th:

Upon inquiry this morning, found there had been a mistake about trains. I should have gone last night, at the same time as the others, as the trains going east and west cross at this point, so I

The CPR branch line, opened in October 1886, facilitated travel between Mattawa and the foot of Lake Temiskaming. Courtesy of the Archives of Ontario, Jones Collection, C147-1-0-2-5 (AO 5618).

will have to wait untill tonight, and miss the train to Sundrich [Sundridge] as well.[40]

Spent most of the day strolling about the streets, and helping Joe Bernard to buy a new suit of clothes.

There is a large amount of business done in Mattawa for the size of the place. Took the train tonight and arrived at Thornecliffe at midnight.

The main street of Mattawa, looking east, as Telfer would have seen it in 1886. Courtesy of the Archives of Ontario, C273-1-0-49-1.

October 15th:

Thornecliffe is a small station on the C.P.R. near La Vase, the terminal of the Muskoka Junction R.R.[41] there are only two or three houses besides the station, one of them doing duty as a hotel.

After breakfasting on potatoes and salt herring, I started out to walk the forty miles to Sundrich, and carry my baggage. Took the railway track, as it is level and dry. The other roads are very wet, owing to the late rain. It is snowing today, and cold and disagreeable. I walked twenty-three miles today, and stopped for the night at one McDonald's, a boarding house full to its utmost capacity.

October 16th:

Last night, Mrs. of the house made a shake-down for me on the floor between the beds, and when I went to look for it, it was not to be found, the men having picked it up and put it on their own bed, so I had to lie down on the bare floor with nothing but my own blanket, and the house was as cold as a barn. I lay shivering all night and got no sleep whatsoever, so I got up around 4 o'clock and started on my journey to keep myself from freezing. About seven o'clock, I went in to a house near the road, got my breakfast, getting some delicious venison, then proceeded down the track.

I reached Sundrich about noon, very tired and sleepy; found a very good hotel kept by J. Young, formerly of Berriedale. After dinner, I felt too stiff and tired to walk into Joly, so concluded to stay overnight. Sundrich, at the present time, has the appearance of growing rapidly, as the majority of the houses appear to be in all different stages of construction. It is a very nice situation, on the north shore of Stony Lake, and a light sandy soil.

October 17th Sunday:

It rained and snowed by turns nearly all day. This, with the deep-rooted aversion to travelling on Sunday, kept me in Sundrich all day. There were quite a number of guests in the house, mostly hunters from the front; one Mr. Lawrence, and two others from Eglinton. [Eglington Post Office was a village on Yonge Street in North York (Toronto) between Eglinton and Lawrence avenues. The Lawrences were an old North York family with several property holdings.] In the evening, I went to the Presbyterian Church, a neat little frame structure, nicely finished and painted inside. It forcibly reminded me of the old frame church where I spent my Sundays when a boy. This one also bore the same name as the old one, the stern old Scottish Reformer, John Knox. There was the same quiet reverence of the congregation to be found only in a rural Presbyterian Church. The singing by the whole congregation of the sacred and time-honoured Psalm of David, and the whole service, brought vividly to my recollection similar scenes of days long gone by where I used to meet with many dear and familiar friends now sleeping in the dust, buried like many of the hopes and aspirations of my boyish days.

October 18th:

Left Sundrich this morning, and went around the east end of Stony Lake, then south on the 30th Side road of Strong, on my way to Joly.

Fount it a very wet road, only fit for travel in winter. The distance from Sundrich to Hartfell is 2 1/2 miles. I stopped at Cunningham's and had dinner.

～

There appear to be no more entries in A.H.Telfer's diary, although there are a few pages cut away after this one; remaining however, is a schedule for the Muskoka Junction Railroad:

North	South
lvs Sundrich 6:30	ar 8:00
" South River 6:57	" 7:35
"Trout Creek 8:00	" 6:43
" Powassan 8:40	" 6:05
" Callendar 9:40	" 5:15
" La Vase 9:55	" 5:00

Alexander Telfer submitted a final report of his own to the Temiscamingue Settlers Association the following year, 1887.

PART THREE

A.H. Telfer's Report to the Temiskaming Settlers' Association – 1887

Report to the President and Members of the Temiscamingue Settlers Association

Gentlemen –

On the morning of the 19th of July 1886, I left Toronto by the morning train on the CPR and joined Mr. Nevin's survey party at Peterboro, and continued the journey to Carleton Junction, from which place after considerable delay we proceeded by the Main Line to Mattawa where we procured our supply of provisions, boats, canoes, etc.; then commenced our arduous journey up the Ottawa River, battling with its terrible rapids, over many of which we had to carry all our stuff, instruments and baggage ammounting to nearly three tons, and in some cases were obliged to carry our boats and canoes as well. This is what makes the voyageur duly thankful for the intervening stretches of smooth water. After three days of rowing, paddling and portaging we arrived at the south end of Lake Temiscamingue, just in time to secure the services of

A photo of the first page of A.H. Telfer's handwritten report. Courtesy of Lorene DiCorpo.

the Steamer Argus to take us up the lake to the Hudson Bay Fort, which is about eighteen or twenty miles from the head of the lake. Here we again transhiped our stuff to our boat and canoes, and proceeded up the lake to Mr. John Piche's farm, our first camping ground on the lands we went to survey. At this point are a gristmill and sawmill which will be a great boon to settlers; and Mr. Piche certainly deserves credit and encouragement for building and maintaining these mills so long in advance of settlement. As it is not necessary to go into a minute account of the incidents of the journey, or the beauties of scenery by lake and river, I will proceed at once to a description of the lands surveyed and fit for settlement.

Our first move was to proceed from our camping ground at the mills down the lake to the north boundary of the township of Loraine previously surveyed, and following that line to the northwest corner of the Township, we ran a line from that point north until we struck the lake again, then returning to the same point we ran a line six miles west, then turned and ran north from that point a distance of twenty four miles; this line composes the western boundary of the townships surveyed in 1886. –

The Ottawa River, and Lake Temiscamingue which is seventy-five miles in length comprise the boundary between Ontario and Quebec, as far as the head of the lake; from that point a line was run due north some sixteen years ago, this is commonly known as the province line. From the western boundary of the land surveyed to this province line is twelve miles, or the width of two townships; we surveyed the boundaries of seven townships, three of which are broken by the lake, the others are six miles square. –

The first township we surveyed, or No. 1 on the plan of survey contains considerable land that is rough and rocky; the rocks are of a dark brown colour and broken up into fragments and square blocks. We passed over several ridges of slate, and by a gradual assent arrived at the summit of the rocks about three quarters of a mile from the northern boundary of the township; this ridge is about one hundred and fifty feet high, and nearly perpendicular on the north side. From this point we enjoyed a splendid view of the country to the north and west, as it lay stretched out at our feet, covered with a carpet of living green. After descending with difficulty the north side of this ridge we entered the fine level tract of country of which the remaining six townships are composed. -

The soil is almost entirely composed of a rich black alluvial mould, varying from six to eighteen inches in depth, this being underlaid by a strong brown clay, thus forming a class of soil for general farming which I believe to be but rarely excelled in the province; there are some places from half a mile to one or two miles in extent where the soil is of a lighter and more sandy nature. This is more specialy the case in portions where the timber has formerly been burnt, and it is now covered with a dense growth of small poplar and spruce. To clear this land for cultivation will require but little labour; other portions are somewhat wet and swampy. Yet these, compared with many of the older settled parts of Ontario would be considered good farming land, and I remember seeing only one place of about half a mile in extent where we found any gravel or stone worth mentioning except on the shore of the lake; and here in a most convenient form and easily accessible, is to be found an abundant supply of limestone. At one point are cliffs over one hundred feet high, and so white as to be plainly seen for miles down the lake. -

The crops we saw growing during our stay in the country were excellent, comprising hay, oats, spring wheat, peas and rye. The growth of potatoes exceeded any I ever saw before, and I was told on good authority that corn grows well and ripens perfectly. Up to the present time the settlers have been able to obtain high prices for their surplus produce from the lumbermen, large numbers of whom have been operating in the country every winter, principally on the Quebec side of the lake. –

The River Blanche is a large and beautifull stream entering the head of the lake from a northwesterly direction, and passing through four of the townships surveyed. At the point where the most northern of these townships crosses, it is ten rods wide and eleven feet deep at low water. This point is about nineteen miles from the mouth, flowing smoothly without the slightest break or rappid, and is navigable for steamers of considerable size. Its banks are wholly composed of clay; the land on either side is good and well timbered. Its waters have generally a whitish appearance owning to the clay through which it flows, hence its name "Blanche," or White River. This stream will doubtless, in the future become a magnificent highway, a source of profit and pleasure to the settlers of that country. –

Another considerable stream called Caticumni, or Wanby's Creek enters that part of the lake called West Bay, flowing through the townships surveyed, and navigable for small boats and canoes for several miles. The land on its banks is good, containing many fine situations for homesteads. –

The timber of this country consists chiefly of pine, cedar, tamarack, spruce, balsam, poplar, white birch and whitewood. Game is not so abundant as in the districts of Muskoka and Parry Sound, yet there are considerable numbers of moose and caribou. Partridges and wild fowl are abundant, as are also the fur-bearing animals; and the waters are well stocked with fish. – There is little doubt that this, as well as other portions of Northern

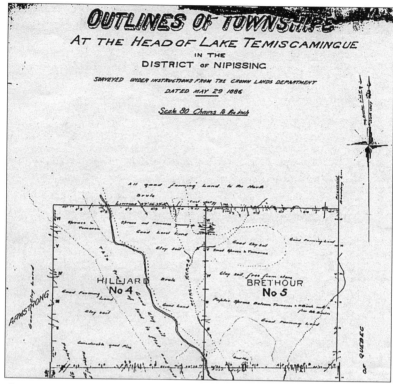

An excerpt from Niven's map of the seven townships outlined,
showing the top of his sketch and Townships 4 & 5 (Hilliard and
Brethour). From Niven, Field Notes. Source: Ontario Ministry of Natural
Resources. Copyright: 2002, Queen's Printer, Ontario.

Ontario, is rich in minerals. A valuable silver mine is now being
worked on the Quebec side of the lake, and similar mines are
known to exist on the Ontario side. –

The rate for freight, per hundred pounds, from Mattawa to the
Hudson's Bay Company's fort is $1.00, passenger fare is about
$4.00, but as there is a prospect of competition during the coming
summer, these rates will probably be lowered. The distance from

the H.B. Fort to the head of the lake is eighteen or twenty miles; here, guides and canoes may be obtained by tourists or explorers who wish to go to the head of the lake or ascend any of the rivers. –

During the summer of 1886 great improvement was made in the travelling facilities of the Upper Ottawa by the Temiscamingue Colonization Society of Quebec who are pushing their enterprise with zeal and energy. Being assisted by their Government by grants of both land and money, they have constructed horse tramways arround the rappids where formerly all freight had to be carried, and small steamers are placed on the smooth water stretches in between. The last rappid, six miles in length and reaching to the south end of Lake Temiscamingue is now overcome by a narrow gauge railway. – The most convenient way to reach this country at present is by the C.P.R. to Mattawa, thence up the Ottawa to Lake Temiscamingue, then by steamer to the H.B. Fort on the head of the lake, and proceed up the Blanche River as far as desired. –

It is well known that a large tract of first class farming land exists, both west and north of the townships already surveyed, and lying in a latitude three degrees south of Winnipeg. It should offer inducements to the intending settler and young men of Ontario, at least equal to those held out by Manitoba and North West, as it is nearer home and the great market centres, and there is room for many thousands of homesteads free from rock or stone. –

In view of these facts it is highly desirable that our Government should open up and place on the market as early as possible this valuable portion of our public domain. –

The construction of the James' Bay Railway would bring this country within easy reach of all parts of Ontario, and I earnestly hope its promoters may receive such encouragement as will enable them to proceed at once with the first eighty miles, reaching the head of Lake Temiscamingue. –

A. H. Telfer
York Mills, May 2nd 1887

Epilogue

An unfinished diary leaves the reader to speculate. Was the foot journey so exhausting, or was it lacking in the novelty of new territories and colourful companions, so that no further comment seemed necessary? Was it a preoccupation with expectations unfulfilled that silenced Telfer's commentary? Such was the denouement of his excursion into the northern bush.

On October 21, 1866, Alexander Niven came to Toronto to settle accounts with the Crown Lands Commissioner and the rest of his crew, having paid some of the men on leaving Mattawa. Estimated final payment to A.H. Telfer was $44.10. Whether this represented all or partial payment is unknown.

The rest of Telfer's life is seen through the writings of his youngest son, Alexander (Sandy) Jefferson Telfer who, like his father, was a diarist. In 1896, Mrs. Mary Jane Telfer passed away after a three-year illness, and the family moved to Niagara Falls,

Ontario, where the eldest son William was working for the Niagara Falls to Buffalo railway. A.H. Telfer apparently did not embark on any other ventures in the north other than hunting expeditions to Haliburton and Muskoka, accompanied by his son Alexander J. who was also developing a love for the northern outdoors.

Between 1904 and 1908, A.H. Telfer's life (he was now in his seventies) took a different turn. During this time he and his brother-in-law Amos Harrington travelled three times to Pinar Del Rio, Cuba. The motivation for such a trip was unclear, but could certainly have included monetary gain and a love of adventure.

Cuba had had its share of turbulent times. Following the Spanish–American War of 1898, U.S. business interests continued to expand in the Caribbean. Competition from European sugar beets had caused the collapse of the Cuban sugar cane market, but the island's economy revived when the U.S. giant, the United Fruit Company, brought about the consolidation of the great banana plantations in Central America and the Caribbean, including Cuba. A.H. Telfer and his brother-in-law might have been investing in the rejuvenation of the sugar business or the expansion of the banana plantations. Relatives and friends back home were being offered investment opportunities at $20 an acre, and for a while, the outlook was positive. It was the heady stuff of dreams, kept alive by the conviction that there was a better life for all if one kept working at it. The dream was never realized, and Alexander H. Telfer died in Niagara Falls on June 27, 1912.

Yet the spirit of adventure lived on. Restless with the pace of life in Niagara Falls and only casual employment opportunities, his son Alexander Jefferson began his travels to Northern Ontario. By rail, foot and canoe he traversed some of the land his father helped to explore - and travelled his own trails as he prospected in the Temagami district, all the while recording events in his diary. As events unfolded, the great northern treasure he would find was not gold, but a wife and family, and home of his own. His father would have approved.

Notes

DEDICATION

1.   Quote by Robert Browning from "Andrea Del Sarto" in *Victorian Poetry*, E.K. Brown, ed. (New York:The Ronald Press, 1942) 243.

PART ONE: HISTORICAL OVERVIEW

1.   For an insightful study of the emigration from the British Isles to 19th century Canada, see Helen I. Cowan's *British Emigration to British North America: The First Hundred Years* (University of Toronto Press, 1961) and T.C. Smout's *A Century of the Scottish People, 1830-1950*. (New Haven:Yale University Press, 1986). See also Lucille H. Campey: *"A Very Fine Class of Immigrants": Prince Edward Island's Scottish Pioneers 1770-1850* (2001); *"Fast Sailing and Copper-Bottomed": Aberdeen Sailing Ships and the Emigrant Scots They Carried to Canada 1774-1855* (2002); *The Silver Chief: Lord Selkirk and the Scottish Pioneers of Belfast, Baldoon and Red River* (2003); and *After the Hector: The Scottish Pioneers of Nova Scotia and Cape Breton* (2004) – all published by Natural Heritage Books,Toronto.

2.   Research on emigrant ships leaving Cromarty in June of 1833 indicates that there were six ships carrying Scottish emigrants bound for Quebec.Young Alexander Telfer and his family sailed on the *Zephyr.* A copy of the receipt of passage dated June 8, 1833, was for the

Zephyr, under Captain Tucker, for a sailing from Cromarty to Quebec departing about the 14th of June. The family of Andrew Telfer was composed of three adults, one under fourteen and three under seven, the third adult likely being his brother William. Total steerage passage, "including Colonial duty" was nine pounds, eight shillings, sixpence.

3.   See Campey, *"Fast Sailing and Copper-Bottomed": Aberdeen Sailing Ships and the Emigrant Scots They Carried to Canada 1774-1855*, 73. Cromarty is to the north of Aberdeen on the east coast. It is likely that Alexander's siblings were victims of cholera. The Quebec Immigration Agent wrote in 1834 that in August of the previous year some 368 Scottish settlers had been unnecessarily detained at Grosse Isle and for too long a time. Having arrived in good health, many came down with cholera. A total of 53 people alter died from the disease during the journey west from Quebec to Prescott (British Parliamentary Papers, 1836 (76) XL).

4.   Edwin C. Guillet, *Pioneer Travel in Upper Canada* (Toronto: Edwin C. Guillet, 1933; University of Toronto Press, 1963) 104-105.

5.   Now known as Knox United Church, the church's congregation celebrated its 150th anniversary in 1998. During the time of the Telfers, agitation for spiritual independence from the parent Church of Scotland, in 1843, was also felt in the colonies. As a result, a group of forty worshippers severed connections with St. Andrew's, the original Presbyterian congregation in Scarborough. Andrew Telfer was one of the founding elders of Knox Presbyterian in 1848. He and his wife Janet, their son Alexander Herkes and his wife Mary Jane are interred in the church cemetery at Midland and Sheppard avenues in Scarborough (Toronto). *Knox Church Scarborough 100th Anniversary* (Agincourt, ON: Knox United Church, 1998) 3-5.

6.   John Muir also emigrated from Scotland in 1833. His son Alexander Muir also was a teacher in the schools of Scarborough and Toronto, but is best known as the composer of the popular patriotic song "The

Maple Leaf Forever." Robert R. Bonis, *A History of Scarborough* (Scarborough: Scarborough Public Library, 1965) 103-104.

7.	This inscription was found in a family collection of books from Scotland.

8.	Thomas Chandler Haliburton, historian and literary humorist, is probably best remembered for his creation of the satirical character "Sam Slick," whose life and times he chronicled in the 1837 book, *The Clockmaker or Sayings and Doings of Samuel Slick of Slickerville.* T.C. Haliburton served as Supreme Court Justice for the Province of Nova Scotia before moving to London in 1842. A staunch Tory, he was a strong believer in free enterprise and individual effort as the key to agricultural and economic development. While in Nova Scotia he used his satiric writing to critique what he believed was a traditional reluctance on the part of Highland Scot settlers and others to work beyond a frugal "make do" philosophy of subsistence farming. Although he never visited the town and county that bear his name today, his company contributed to the development of the district, surveying the town plot for Haliburton and opening the first store and post office there in 1864. The company also donated the site for St. George's Anglican Church in 1865, the year Haliburton died. In his memory his wife, Sarah, he donated an organ to the church. Rotary Club of Haliburton, *Haliburton Village 1864-1964.* (Haliburton: Rotary Club of Haliburton, 1964) 5. See also Graeme Wynn, "On the Margins of Empire 1760-1840," in *The Illustrated History of Canada*, Craig Brown, ed. (Toronto: Lester Publishing Ltd., 1991) 244-245.

9.	The Canadian Land and Emigration Company was created in 1862 by a consortium of English businessmen under the chairmanship of T.C. Haliburton. A block of Crown Land in the District of Haliburton was up for sale and the Company purchased some 360,000 acres, the equivalent of ten adjoining townships: Havelock, Eyre, Clyde, Bruton, Harburn, Guilford, Dysart, Dudley, Harcourt and Langford. Over a period of eighty years the company was sold and reconfigured. By 1946 all of the original land holdings had been sold, and the company ceased operations permanently. Trent University Archives, Canadian Land and Emigration Company collection. (http://www.trentu.ca/library/archives/77-023.htm)

10.   The Provisional County of Haliburton was created in 1874 by special act of the Provincial Government, when Oliver Mowat was Premier. This act of separation from Peterborough and Victoria counties was to facilitate the financing of the Victoria Railway to be laid between Lindsay and Haliburton. Under Warden Alexander Niven, the Council passed a bylaw granting $55,000 towards the railway's construction. The line officially opened in November 1878. H.R. Cummings, *Early Days in Haliburton* (Haliburton: Haliburton Highlands Museum, 1993) 157.

11.   See Robert C. Lee, *The Canada Company and the Huron Tract 1826-1853: Personalities, Profits and Politics* (Toronto: Natural Heritage, 2004).

12.   Surveying uses the global measurement systems of longitude and latitude as the basis for the assessment of smaller areas of land. Meridians of longitude are imaginary circles around the earth passing through and converging at the poles and pointing to true north. Parallels of latitude circle the earth in an east-west direction parallel to the equator. In determining the line of a principal north-south meridian, a surveyor would thus create an initial point from which to run an east-west base line (at right angle), to then be used as a benchmark measurement for the creation of other lines delineating township divisions. From John Ladell, *They Made Their Mark: Surveyors and Their Role in the Settlement of Ontario* (Toronto: Downtown Press, 1993) 16.

13.   The Native individual, Bernard, is probably the same man referred to throughout the diary as Joe Bernard. From local accounts, his name was actually Bernard Naraseau, from the Lac des Deux Montagnes area near Montreal. He maintained a home in Haliburton and worked

frequently for Niven as a canoeman. Leopolda z L. Dobrzenski, *Fragments of a Dream: Pioneering in Dysart Township and Haliburton Village* (Haliburton, Ontario: Municipality of Dysart, 1985).

14. These seven townships would eventually be identified as Bucke, Dymond, Harley, Hilliard, Brethour, Casey and Harris.

15. An historic plaque stands beside Highway 11 where it crosses Niven's Meridian, about three km west of the town of Cochrane. Alexander Niven began the first phase of his exploration line from the northeast corner of Lumsden Township, northwest of Sudbury, and ran the line 193 km due north to the approximate latitude of present-day Timmins. In 1898, Niven continued the line to a point about 30 miles from the site of the town of Moosonee, establishing the only major meridian in Ontario to reach salt water. John Ladell, *They Left Their Mark*, 214.

16. Association of Ontario Land Surveyors, *Annual Report*. No. 26, 1911, 11-12.

17. George L. Cassidy, *Arrow North: The Story of Temiskaming* (Cobalt, Ontario: Highway Book Shop, 1976) 64-65.

18. Over the years several fortified trading posts were constructed at or near the site of Fort Temiscamingue, on the east shore of Lake Temiscamingue, near present-day Ville Marie, Quebec. The earliest to be named Fort Temiscamingue was established in the 17th century, but was short-lived. In 1720, a Montreal merchant named Paul Guillet received a license to trade and he re-established the fort. In the competition for furs, the fort was taken over in turn by the North West (NWC) and the Hudson's Bay (HBC) companies. By the late 19th century, declining fur stocks, largely due to over-trapping and the coming of the CPR east/west line caused the HBC to move its local operations headquarters to Mattawa House at the confluence of the Ottawa and

Mattawa rivers in 1882. The old fort was eventually abandoned in 1901. Government of Canada, *Fort Temiscamingue National Historic Site* (Ottawa: Environment Canada Parks Service, 1989) 2. See also the following excerpt about Fort Temiskamingue from Bruce W. Taylor's unpublished guide to "Historic Sites in Temiskaming":

"French traders erected the first trading post on Lake Temiskaming in 1679 on Meadow Island at the mouth of the Montreal River. This island has since been flooded due to construction of a power dam at Temiscamigue, Quebec, in 1917. Sieur de Troyes, a French soldier, stayed at this fort for several days in 1686 while on his way to James Bay to capture the English forts there. Two years later, marauding Iroquois from New York State captured and burned the fort with the loss of several French traders. The fort and trading post were then moved to the present location at the narrows opposite the Old Mission, but because of the continuing Iroquois threat, it became inactive, and the Native people were forced to trade their furs on Lake Nipissing, or on the lower Ottawa River.

Today, as one looks out over the waters of Lake Temiskaming where the Montreal River enters the lake, there is nothing to indicate that there was once a major trading post there. No markers exist on the shore to remind one that three hundred years ago Algonquins and their French allies fought to the death here against war-like Iroquois invaders.

It was not until 1720, after the Iroquois had been defeated, that the post was re-established by Montreal traders. After the conquest of 1759, the fort was operated by independent English and Scots traders until 1787 when the North West Company was established and took over. With the merger of the North West Company (NWC) and the Hudson's Bay Company (HBC) in 1821, the fort, now a major trading and supply centre, was operated by the latter company until encroaching civilization forced its closure in 1887."

For information on the Old Mission, see the following excerpt from Bruce W. Taylor's unpublished guide to "Historic sites in Temiskaming":

The Temiskaming Mission (Old Mission)

"A sign indicates a left turn for the "Temiskaming Mission." The road from the highway into the mission is a narrow gravel road that is privately maintained, but the four-kilometre drive along the birch-lined road is worth the effort, and the view from the Mission is interesting from a historical perspective. The site of the Old Mission is marked by a historic plaque and also a large wooden cross erected by a local francophone historical group. You can park your vehicle at the plaque and walk down to the shore of Lake Temiskaming, where you will see directly across the narrows, on the Quebec shore, the site of Old Fort Temiskaming.

Many local historians point to the Old Mission as the most historic site on Lake Temiskaming. On August 15, 1966, the Government of Canada installed a commemorative plaque, recognizing the historical importance of the site. Most of the site is now in private hands and in danger of being lost to development.

In 1863, priests of the Oblate Order of the Roman Catholic Church, assisted by Algonquin natives and employees of the HBC fort, constructed a rough dwelling at Mission Point, across the narrows from the fort, thus establishing the first mission. A year later, Mgr. Eugène-Bruno Guigues, Bishop of Ottawa, became the first bishop to visit Lake Temiskaming, and gave the mission the name "Mission Saint Claude." The following year a small chapel was constructed.

Realizing that there were problems with health, education and the protection of orphans, the Oblates requested that the Grey Nuns of Ottawa establish a presence to operate a school and hospital. In 1866, two nuns of that order arrived at the mission and began their work. The first hospital was erected by December, 1866, and an orphanage and school established the following year.

The energetic Oblates also operated three farms: one at the mission proper, where potatoes were grown and cows and sheep kept; a second in a clearing about two miles south of the mission, where produce was grown; and a third at Tête du Lac (North Temiskaming), where marsh hay was gathered as feed for the livestock.

In 1874, a fourth farm was established across the lake at Baie-des-Pères (Ville Marie), with a proper barn and stable. It was to this location that the mission was eventually moved in 1887 when the situation on Lake Temiskaming had changed due to the closing of Fort Temiskaming, the encroachment of civilization and settlement of the Quebec shore, and the establishment of an Indian reserve at the mouth of the Quinze River.

Some of the mission buildings were dismantled, some were moved in later years to Ville Marie or to the Wright Mine in Quebec, and some were left to gradually fade away. In 1906, 1280 acres owned by the Oblates was sold to J.D. McLaren, who established a farm on the mission site. All that was retained by the Oblates was two acres of land on which the mission church once stood.

The historical significance of Fort Temiskaming across the narrows on the Quebec shore will be dealt with later; but it is worth noting here that geographical features on the shores of the lake are replete with names that reflect the long history of the fur trade. For example, the point of land approximately four kilometres south of the mission is named "Pointe à la Barbe," or "Beard Point." The point is so named because the voyageurs in the canoe brigades arriving from the south would stop at this point to shave and clean up before making their approach to Fort Temiskaming."

19. *Report to the Commissioner of Crown Lands, 1886.* The land in question – the Clay Belt – lay not only in the seven townships surveyed around the head of the lake but included the area to the north covered by the watershed of the Blanche River and its tributaries.

20. A.H. Telfer, *Report to the Temiskaming Settlers' Association, 1886.*

21. The Cochrane (Great) and Little Claybelt (Temiskaming) extended across Ontario and Quebec. The Ontario portion consisted of 16,600,000 acres. Although squatters used land around the lake's edge for hunting camps and trading centres, former Hudson's Bay factor,

C.C. Farr purchased recently surveyed land at Humphrey's Depot and erected his new home there in 1890. George L. Cassidy, *Arrow North: The Story of Temiskaming*, 105.

22. J. Brian Bird, *The Natural Landscapes of Canada: A Study in Regional Earth Science* (Toronto: John Wiley and Sons Canada, 1980) 61.

23. The settlements of Cobalt, Kirkland Lake and New Liskeard would owe their existence to the wealth of local mineral deposits. Today depleted resources and competition from other markets have left these hardy northern towns economically depressed. For a colourful and detailed history of the area see Peter Fancy's *Silver Centre: The Story of a Mining Camp and Temiskaming Treasure Trails, The Earliest Years* (Cobalt: Highway Book Shop, 1992). See also the following excerpt from Bruce W. Taylor, *New Liskeard: The Pioneer Years* (Cobalt: Highway Book Shop, 1933).

(New Liskeard) The Pioneers 1891-92

"At first glance it would appear that the first two settlers to set foot on the muddy bank of the Wabi River (where the town of New Liskeard stands now), in June 1891, were an odd couple. William Murray, 60 years old, an Anglican, was paddling in the bow of their borrowed canoe, while the youngster, Irvin Heard, 29 years old, a Presbyterian, paddled in the stern.[1] *(From Everett Heard, personal interview, Englehart, Ont., December 13, 1993. Irvin Heard's son, Everett, indicated to the author that because Murray, in the bow of the canoe, was the eldest, and was the first to set foot on shore, he got first pick and chose the 320 acre farm closest to Lake Temiskaming. Irvin Heard chose the next farm to the west.)*

In fact, they had much in common. Both hailed from the Haliburton area of central Ontario. Murray from the town of Haliburton itself, where he had worked as a forest ranger and guide, and developed a love of the wilderness; Heard was from the town of Minden in Haliburton County.

Both were bachelors; both had worked on survey parties north of Lake Temiskaming in 1887 and 1889. Both formed such an attraction for the north country that they intended to settle here.

The two men had arranged between themselves that they would each claim a farm lot of 320 acres at the mouth of the Wabi River, with the senior, Murray, getting first pick of the lots. Having both previously worked on survey crews in Temiskaming, they knew exactly where to find the concession line and the corner posts. They settled on lots 8 and 9 in the second concession, Dymond Township, with Murray claiming lot 9, at the mouth of the river, while Heard claimed the next one to the west. The marker delineating the boundary between the two lots lies in the vicinity of the present-day post office.

Both men cleared parts of their land that year and built log cabins. The following year, Murray sent for his half sister, Charlotte Rebecca (Lottie) Beavis, who joined him that year. Another half-sister, Annie Catherine Beavis, joined them later.

Irvin Heard lived alone on his farm until 1906 when he married Arvilla Latchford. In a deposition relating to a lawsuit in 1903, he stated that except for William Murray there was no other settler within six miles for the first year he lived here. He became embroiled in 1903 in a dispute with Crown Lands Agent John Armstrong over ownership of the land that he had claimed. He eventually sold his holdings and moved to Southern Ontario in 1916. Fourteen years later, in 1930, he returned to the north and purchased a farm near Charlton where he farmed until his death on June 21, 1956.

It is ironic that William Murray and Irvin Heard, the first two men who established farms at what later became known as New Liskeard, are remembered in quite different ways. William Murray became known as a "Founding Father" of the town, (along with the Crown Lands Agent, John Armstrong, who arrived in 1894). Murray died on October 26, 1906, and is buried at Haliburton. Irvin Heard's part in the settlement of New Liskeard has been largely ignored by previous histories, and he is rarely given credit for being a pioneer in the town of New Liskeard. Except for having streets named for them, there are no monuments to either man in New Liskeard and, in fact, no gravestone marked Heard's final resting place in the cemetery at Charlton until the late 1990s.

The Lake Temiskaming area was certainly not unknown to Europeans in the 19th century. The area had been mapped as early as 1686, when Sieur de Troyes made his famous expedition from Montreal through Temiskaming to attack the English forts at James Bay. Prior to 1759, French fur traders travelled up the Ottawa River from Montreal to trade with the Algonquin Indians, and established Fort Temiskaming as a trading post. Later fur traders associated with the Hudson's Bay Company (HBC), and the North West Company (NWC) came south from Hudson Bay, as well as up the Ottawa River route. Lumbermen also, made their way up the Ottawa River, and were cutting pine on Lake Temiskaming by the middle of the 19th century. Missionaries of the Roman Catholic Church were active among the Natives in the area over the years, but it was not until 1863 that a permanent presence was established by the Oblate Order at Mission St. Claude (Temiskaming Mission) at the narrows on Lake Temiskaming, directly across the lake from Fort Temiskaming. One of the reasons why the area did not attract large numbers of settlers until almost the turn of the century, was the difficulty in accessing the area.

Prior to 1882, when the CPR Railway reached Mattawa, access on the upper Ottawa River was via small steamboats. with many portages. The coming of the railway made the journey to Mattawa much easier. However, north of Mattawa, the Ottawa River contained four major sets of rapids; La Cave Rapids, Les Erables Rapids, La Montagne Rapids and the six-mile-long Long Sault Rapids, located just south of Temiscamingue, Quebec, at the south end of Lake Temiskaming. At first, traffic into Lake Temiskaming was by canoe, with portages around the rapids. The Roman Catholic Church, in their efforts to attract French-Canadian settlers to the Quebec shore of Lake Temiskaming, gradually improved the route by installing small steamboats between the rapids, and building narrow gauge railways over the portages. Dubbed the "Moccasin Express," this access was taken over by the CPR who completed a branch line from Mattawa to Temiscamingue (or Gordon Creek as it was then known) in 1895.

The Quebec shore of Lake Temiskaming was settled first. The first official settler took up land near present-day Ville Marie in 1882, but it was not until access was improved that a flood of settlers arrived in the 1890s.

On the Ontario shore of the lake, the first settler was the ex-Hudson's Bay Company employee, Charles Cobbold (C.C.) Farr, who, in 1885, acquired a piece of land at the Lake Temiskaming terminus of the age-old Matabanik Portage (or Humphrey's Landing, as it was also known) into the Montreal River. Farr resigned from the HBC in 1889, moved his family to his property, and commenced to start a town which he called "Haileybury" after his school in England. There were a few other settlers, mostly ex-lumbermen or squatters who trapped or cut marsh hay for the lumber camps, but Farr was the first "colonizer" in what was widely known as "New Ontario." He wrote several pamphlets encouraging settlement, and was a tireless promoter of the area.

Irvin Heard

The Heard family has roots in Temiskaming as deep, or deeper than any other non-Native family. When Irvin Heard joined William Murray in his land-staking trip in June 1891, he was only one of several of the family who had already taken up land, or had been involved in some aspect of opening up the wilderness that was Temiskaming. Thus, it is somewhat ironic that the Heard name while occasionally mentioned in early histories of the area, is not referred to as being a "founding" family.[2] *(The name has been spelled "Heard" or "Hurd," sometimes interchangeably. The more common form "Heard" is the spelling of choice here.)*

Irvin Heard was born on October 9, 1871,[3] *(Most of the details and specific dates regarding this family came from an interview by the author with Everett Heard, the only son of Irvin Heard, in Englehart, December 13, 1993. Other dates (birth dates) have been gleaned from the 1901 census.)* at Minden, Haliburton County, Ontario. The Heard family originated in the border country between England and Scotland. Irvin's grandfather, Rob Roy Heard, and his wife, Jane Rutherford, brought their family out to Canada in the 1850s, and settled in the Port Hope/Coburg area. In 1862, Irvin's father, William Robert Heard and his wife Loretta Bullock purchased a farm near Minden from the Canadian Land and Immigration Company (a company notorious for purchasing marginal or poor land from the government and reselling it to unsuspecting immigrants). Irvin, his seven brothers and one sister grew up on the farm at Minden, but obviously young Irvin suffered from wanderlust as he at the age of 16, along with his uncle James Heard, joined a survey party in Temiskaming in 1887.[4] *(Everett Heard told the author that James Heard owned a pair of oxen, which he drove up to Lake Temiskaming. The oxen were named Bucke and Dymond, and the Townships of Bucke and Dymond were named for these oxen. This myth has made its way into several histories including "Fragments of a Dream," a history of Haliburton. The official, less romantic origin of these names is that Bucke Township (which includes the Town of Haileybury) was named for Dr. Richard Maurice Bucke, Medical Superintendent, London, Ontario, and Dymond Township (New Liskeard) was named for A.H. Dymond, Principal of the Blind Institute, Brantford, Ontario.)*

After working for the season on the survey crew, Irvin went back to Haliburton, where the family had relocated in 1862, but he had been impressed enough with the area around Lake Temiskaming that he was determined to return and claim some of the good farmland. There is some indication that James Heard may have stayed for a year at Haileybury before returning to Minden. A surveyor, C.D. Bowman, who surveyed the boundaries of Bucke Township in 1887, indicates on his map that besides a Mr. Humphry (the site was originally known as Humphry's Landing) there were two other settlers, J. Moore and J. Hurd.

During the winter of 1891, Irvin, and his uncles James and Andrew walked on the ice from Temiscaming, Quebec, up the lake as far as Fort Temiskaming. Andrew somehow got wet and developed pneumonia along the way. He died at Fort Temiskaming, the old Hudson's Bay Company fur trading post, where he was buried in the Protestant cemetery. Irvin and James carried on and arrived at Haileybury on April 10, 1891.

During his stay at Haileybury, Irvin Heard worked for a time for C.C. Farr as a teamster, driving supplies over the Matabanik Trail from Haileybury to the Montreal River.[5] *(Interview, December 13, 1993. Everett Heard said that his father worked for a year as a teamster for C.C. Farr. It is possible (but not very likely) that he stayed after the survey crew of 1887 was disbanded and worked for a year then, however, it is more likely that he worked for Farr from April 10, 1891 until he paddled with Murray to the Wabi River in June of that year.)* Farr had resigned his position with the Hudson's Bay Company in 1889 and, by 1891, had moved his family to Haileybury and was actively encouraging settlement.

When Irvin Heard and William Murray pulled their canoe up on the muddy banks of the Wabi River in June 1891, Heard was on a mission for other members of his family. He was to have scouted out the area for his father and his uncles, and if possible locate farms for them. He was able to locate a 320 acre farm for his own account, and almost certainly would have reported on the favourable conditions to his uncle in Haileybury.

The lot that Irvin Heard located was lot no. 8, concession 2, Township of Dymond, the lot immediately to the west of that of William Murray.[6] *(Heard was later to say that while William Murray was the first settler in New Liskeard, the (Heard) was the first settler in Dymond Township. In actual fact, the Brooks family were the first settlers in Dymond, arriving in 1891.)* The Wabi River bisects this lot diagonally from southwest to northeast, and the land, while cut in places from gullies running into the river, is generally good well-drained farm land. Heard erected a log home on the north half of the lot (north of the river), and over the next few years, cleared some forty-five acres, slashed another five acres, and built a second house, two barns, as well as stables and other outbuildings. In the fall of 1891, since there was no Crown Lands Agent in Temiskaming, he notified the Crown Lands Department at Toronto that he had settled on the lot, and wished to purchase it when the lots came up for sale. He received acknowledgment of his application at that time.

What happened next raises some serious questions about John

Armstrong's motives and integrity when he was appointed Crown Lands Agent in 1894, particularly in his dealings with Irvin Heard.

When Heard and Murray staked their claims to farms in 1891, it was understood (and was government policy), that each settler could claim 320 acres. When John Armstrong started his duties as Crown Lands Agent in 1894, he recognized, quite rightly, that unless the acreage was decreased, it would be a long time before the country would be developed, and the population would not support a centre such as New Liskeard or Haileybury. He arranged to have the acreage halved to 160 acres for each settler. The *New Liskeard Speaker* [of June 30, 1927] explained the situation thus: [7] *(The Speaker is in error here, as the revised acreage was 160 acres.)*

"It will be of interest to later arrivals, and more especially to those who now cannot purchase more than 80 acres,[7] to know that the first purchasers of Crown Land in Temiskaming were allowed a full lot of 320 acres each. But the agent saw that if this wholesale method of selling so much land to each purchaser were to continue the country would be sparsely settled and that many years would elapse ere the land would be cleared. Representations were made to the Department of Lands, and the change was made allowing one purchaser only one-half section only.

Soon after the change was made, however, there was "trouble in the camp." Newcomers did not take kindly to the idea of being restricted to only half the land first-comers had, and decided that it were better that all should be treated alike. In order to give effect to their views, they petitioned the Minister of Lands to compel those holding 320 acres to give up half their land. The Hon. E.J. Davis had become Crown Lands Commissioner by this time. He decided that the first arrivals in Temiskaming who had purchased full lots in good faith should be allowed to retain this land.

In the early days, when there were no roads, it will be understood it was of great advantage to a farmer to have his home as close to New Liskeard as possible, and that if all those who held 320 acres each had to give up half a section this would enable more farmers to get land where there were roads.

And there was also a little friction caused by "land-jumpers" or "squatters," a number of men who would settle on land which the owner had temporarily vacated while on a business trip or a visit to his old home in the south. But public opinion did not sympathize with the squatters nor did the government recognize their claims."

In 1894, John Armstrong petitioned the Ontario government to allow him a "free grant" of lands which included the south half of lots 7 and 8 in Dymond Township. In reply, Aubrey White, Assistant Commissioner, in a letter dated July 17, 1894, informed Armstrong that, "... the lands in said township (Dymond) have been placed on the market for sale by order of council. It is impossible to make a free grant to you, but if you desire to purchase the said land under the ordinary conditions, an Order in Council can probably be obtained."[8] *(Letter from Assistant Commissioner Aubrey White to John Armstrong, July 17, 1894. Exhibit "B" in Land Titles Act dispute dated February 17, 1904.)*

What Mr. White could not have known, but John Armstrong certainly would have known, was that Irvin Heard had, three years previously, claimed this lot as his own.

On December 24, 1894, Assistant Commissioner White informed Armstrong in a letter that, "... by Order in Council, dated 18th inst., you are allowed to purchase the south halves of lots 7 and 8 in the 2nd Con. of Dymond at 50 cents an acre, 317 acres, subject to settlement and pine tree regulations."[9] *(Letter from Assistant Commissioner Aubrey White to John Armstrong, December 24, 1894. Exhibit "A.")*

Irvin Heard's reaction to this encroachment on land that he understood to be his was predictable. In his deposition, dated December 23, 1903, before a Notary Public, he stated:

About five years after I had settled on said lot, John Armstrong, the Crown Lands Agent for the Temiskaming District arrived in the fall of the year and went out and returned again in the following spring.

When the said John Armstrong first came to the district, he informed me that he had applied for and purchased from the government the part of said lot (Lot 8) lying south of the Wahbie River which was a matter of great surprise to me as I had been in actual possession of the whole lot for about five years. I then made the necessary affidavits before the same John Armstrong and applied for all that part of the lot lying north of the said Wahbie River. It was then distinctly understood and agreed upon between the said John Armstrong and myself that the Wahbie River should be the boundary line between us.

Heard's deposition went on to state that Armstrong came back the following spring and erected a shanty on the part of lot 8 lying south of the river, but never actually lived there (contrary to the terms of settlement), and never made any improvements to the land, i.e. clearing or cultivation etc.

One must remember that Irvin Heard, in 1894, was only 23 years old, and would be no match for the 45-year-old Armstrong who was experienced in the rough and tumble political arena of Muskoka. Heard appears to have surrendered his interest in the part of the lot lying south of the river (later to become a residential area in New Liskeard), and retreated to the part north of the river.

Armstrong, however, was not satisfied with prying the south bank away from Heard, and also applied for, and received title to a strip of land along the north bank of the river, on the pretence that the agreement between himself and Heard was for Heard to surrender one-half of the lot, which would include land north of the river.

Heard, in his deposition, states clearly that Armstrong did not make any claim to this lot until Heard himself applied for a patent, and that Armstrong was well aware that Heard had lived on and had been farming the land in question. Also, according to Heard, Armstrong had offered to buy the land north of the river, but Heard refused. The outcome of the suit was that Armstrong retained title to a 37 acre strip of land along the river, which later became valuable residential land. Head was left with the north half of the lot, which, while eventually subdivided into lots, was not nearly as valuable.

It is interesting that Heard was able to enlist the assistance of Thomas McCamus and George Taylor, two highly respected residents of the town. McCamus, a partner with Angus McKelvie in the town's only sawmill (at that time), and George Taylor, hardware merchant and ex-mayor of London, Ontario, posted affidavits in support of Heard.

Irvin Heard continued to live on his land, and was able to participate in the land boom to the extent that he had part of his land subdivided and sold, starting in 1905. In 1906, he married Arvilla Latchford. The couple had two children, Osborne, who died as a child, and Everett, born October 14, 1913. Heard suffered the loss of his home in November, 1910, when it burned to the ground. The *New Liskeard Speaker* of February 3, 1910, reported that nothing could be saved, and that fire fighting was hampered by "cartridges exploding in all directions."

The lot that Heard retained includes the land later occupied by the Government Demonstration Farm, and later the New Liskeard Agricultural College. When the New Liskeard Agricultural Society was first established, Heard sold them a parcel of land that became New Liskeard's first fair grounds. In 1916, Heard sold a large parcel of his remaining land to Adelard Maille, one of the first French-Canadian residents in New Liskeard. He then spent a number of years farming in various southern Ontario locations, returning periodically to New Liskeard where most of his immediate family now lived. According to Everett Heard, his father farmed at Burford, Ontario, Darling Road (near Caledonia), Mount Vernon, Brantford, and Scarborough. He returned to New Liskeard for a year in 1918, and again in 1923, when he worked for the Hill, Clark & Francis planing mill.

In 1930, Heard purchased a 32 acre farm about one mile west of the village of Charlton. He lived there, and farmed that land and another 160-acre lot that he purchased up the "North Road" near Charlton. Irvin

Heard died in Charlton on June 21, 1956. His wife, Arvilla had passed away in March 1947. Both are buried in the Charlton Cemetery.

As noted earlier in this chapter, the Heard family in addition to being pioneers in Haliburton County, have deep roots in Temiskaming. Irvin, his uncle James, and possibly other uncles, worked on the government surveys in Temiskaming as early as 1887. Irvin's uncle, Andrew, died of pneumonia on the trip up Lake Temiskaming in 1891, and is buried in the Protestant cemetery at Fort Temiskaming. James and Margaret Carr, were the first couple to be married in New Liskeard.[10] *(James and Margaret Carr were married on July 11, 1894 in the William Murray's home, in an Anglican ceremony presided over by Rev. Johnston of Haileybury.)* A cousin, Rob Roy Heard (son of Joseph Heard and Jane Sawyer), and Maria Fernholm, the daughter of one of the original Swedish settlers in Bucke Township, were only the fourth couple to be married in the Presbyterian Church in New Liskeard. Rob Roy Heard took up prospecting after the silver rush at Cobalt started, and later moved to Swastika. He disappeared in the bush while on a prospecting expedition, and was never found.

Irvin Heard's parents, William Robert Heard, and Loretta Bullock had eight children besides Irvin, and most settled in Temiskaming. The 1901 census lists the following children as living with William Heard in Dymond Township: William (born 24/03/1874), Frank (born 12/04/1882), Arthur (born 08/03/1883), Allan (born 22/07/1886) and James A. (born 05/08/1887). Not listed in the 1901 census are: Emma (Tripp), George, and Andrew.[11] *(For more information see,* Fragments of a Dream: Pioneering in Dysart Township and Haliburton Village, *by Leopolda z L. Dobrzensky, published by the Municipality of Dysart, 1985.)*

24. *Northern Districts of Ontario: Eastern Algoma, Northern Nipissing, Rainy River and Temiskaming* [prepared under instructions from Hon. A.S. Hardy, Commissioner of Crown Lands] (Toronto: Warwick Brothers and Rutter, 1895) 60.

25. Richard Tatley, *Northern Steamboats: Timiskaming, Nipissing & Abitibi* (Erin, Ontario: Boston Mills Press, 1995) 73-80.

26. Haileybury (Matabanick) (Humphrey's Landing) With a current population of 47,000, Haileybury is located in Bucke Township, on Lake Temiskaming, and is situated on the lake. Cassidy, *Arrow North*, 240-248. See also an excerpt from Bruce W. Taylor, *Place Names of Temiskaming*. New Liskeard, Ont.: White Mountain Publications, 2000.

Haileybury is at the Temiskaming terminus of an ancient portage into Portage Bay on the Montreal River. It was once known as "Matabanick" and also as "Humphrey's Landing." The community was established by a former Hudson's Bay Company trader, Charles Cobbold (C.C.) Farr, who purchased land at that location in 1883. Farr built a home in 1889 and naming the fledgling settlement Haileybury, after his old school in England. The first post office in Temiskaming was established at Haileybury in 1890, and the first Anglican Church services were held as early as 1894, although the church was not built until 1896. The first public school was established in 1894. The town grew slowly until the discovery of silver at Cobalt in 1903 resulted in an explosion of population. Many miners and mine officials established homes in Haileybury and, by 1906, the town boasted three large elegant hotels, brokerages and many other businesses. A disastrous fire in 1906 levelled much of the business section, but was it was quickly rebuilt.

When the District of Temiskaming was formed in 1912, Haileybury was declared the District Seat, and became home to the District Court House, the Jail and the Land Titles Office.

The great fire of 1922 (sometimes called the Great Haileybury Fire – although it caused widespread devastation throughout Temiskaming) was of a more serious nature. Virtually the entire town was destroyed, and there were 12 fatalities.

The waterfront at Haileybury was the location of a large dock and warehouse complex, and a farmers' market that was a busy place during the steamboat era on Lake Temiskaming. In 1924, the first scheduled air mail service in Canada was inaugurated between Haileybury and Rouyn, Quebec. Haileybury is also the location of the world-famous Haileybury School of Mines.

27.   The dividing line between "Old" and "New" Ontario followed the old voyageur river route of the Ottawa, Mattawa and French rivers.

28.   Alexander Niven and his fellow surveyors of the North Shore of Georgian Bay (Francis Bolger, Frank Purvis, Elihu Stewart, Thomas Speight) found much of the land "as a whole unfitted for agricultural purposes." Ladell, *They Left Their Mark*, 179.

29.   The economic future of the Sudbury District would inevitably be tied to the mining of nickel, copper and precious metals, and to the Canadian Pacific Railway which provided direct access to the area. Farming also expanded into a long fertile valley to the north of the city, within the bowl of the ore-bearing Sudbury Basin. Mining and smelting continue to drive the economy although in a lesser way as the city is a hub for higher education and medical facilities for the north-central part of the province. Environmental programs have allowed for the renewal and regeneration of local forests and wildlife habitats, for years denuded by the effects of sulphur dioxide emissions.

30.   In 1937 a memorial tablet was erected at the Parliament Buildings in Toronto by the Association of Ontario Land Surveyors (AOLS) and the Government of Ontario. It commemorates the founding of the AOLS and honours the early surveyors who were instrumental in bringing about the orderly settlement of the province. W.F. Weaver, "Ontario Surveys and the Land Surveyor," *Canadian Geographical Journal, 1946*, 189.

31.   Cadastral surveys, more commonly known as "Legal surveys," determined the size and location of parcels of land for the purpose of sale or evaluation. Those with the greatest vested interest in the land – settlers, lumbermen, prospectors – would have benefitted from topographic information; however, financial support from the government could only provide for limited cadastral surveys, albeit at little or no expense to the original settlers. It was not until 1904 that topographical

survey agencies were first set up. L.M. Sebert, "The Land Surveys of Ontario 1750-1980," *Cartographica.* Vol. 17. No. 3. 1980, 8.

32. Niven's field notes are on file at the offices of the Ministry of Natural Resources in Peterborough, Ontario, and, beyond their technical data, they provide an interesting account of the rugged life and travels of surveyors in the 19th century.

33. Leopolda z L. Dobrzenski, *Fragments of a Dream: Pioneering in Dysart Township and Haliburton Village.* (Peterborough, Ont.: Heritage Publishing Ltd., 1985) 39-40.

PART TWO: THE DIARY OF A.H. TELFER – 1886

1.   A.H. Telfer travelled from his York Mills home via stagecoach to the CPR station. As the line did not pass through the city proper south of Bloor Street (the Grand Trunk Railway ran near the lakeshore), he probably made his way to the station at Agincourt, the neighbourhood of his youth.

2.   Peterborough, in Peterborough County, the crew's first meeting point, was becoming a regional lumbering and agricultural centre. The swampy land observed from the train could have been related to the town's low-lying site on the west bank of the Otonabee River.

3.   The party began the ascent of the Ottawa River at Mattawa, a town built first on the fur trade, then on lumber. In 1837, the Hudson's Bay Company established a permanent fur trading post known as Mattawa House (not to be confused with a hotel of the same name erected around that time). When Niven's party arrived in 1886, Mattawa had been formally incorporated as a village for two years. The CPR had come in 1881, and with it an influx of settlers and entrepreneurs so that the town became a major supplier to the lumber trade. Although there would have been little time for sightseeing, the men would have remarked at several prominent structures such as the town hall and fire hall. Gerard Therrien has written a colourful local history entitled *Mattawa: Our Timeless Town* (Mattawa, Ontario; Canadian Millennium Partnership Program and the Mattawa Historical Society, 1999). For further background and photos, see Leo Morel, *Mattawa: The Meeting of the Waters* (Mattawa, Ontario: Société historique de Mattawa, 1980); and *Canadian Pacific Railway Station: Mattawa, Ontario* (Hull, Quebec: Historic Sites and Monuments Board of Canada) RSR-17.

4.   According to Niven's field notes, these four were John Soucy, Joseph Bernard, John Gagnon and a Native man, Perrault. Joseph Bernard, a Native of Lac des Deux Montagnes near Montreal, came

regularly to the Haliburton area to hunt. Niven knew him as an experienced canoeman and employed his services. Cummings, *Early Days in Haliburton*, 49.

5.   Over a distance of fifteen miles the traveller would encounter daunting rapids at La Cave, Les Erables and La Montagne; Les Erables was considered the most hazardous.

6.   The Long Sault was a series of six rapids over a distance of as many miles.

7.   In his report to the Temiskamingue Settlers' Association, A.H. Telfer identified the steamer as the "Argus," which in fact was the *Argo*. Built at Temiskaming in 1882, the *Argo* was a double-decked sidewheel tug, 125 feet in length, at that time owned by northern entrepreneur Alex Lumsden. Lumsden, born in 1844 in Ottawa, learned the sawyer's trade as a young man and went on the start a lumber business of his own, eventually becoming one of the leading logging contractors on the Ottawa River. He also purchased steamboats (the *Argo* was his first) to tow his huge log booms down Lake Temiskaming and into the Ottawa River, while employing some in the passenger trade on the Lake. A popular businessman, he was elected as MLA in Ottawa in 1898. He died a very wealthy man in 1904. The *Argo* served the lumber trade, towing rafts, scows and log booms, as well as transporting men, provisions and horses until she was finally sold in 1920 and dismantled. The indomitable tug was to live on, as her massive engine was salvaged and installed in a larger, steel-hulled vessel. For a history of steamboating on Lake Temiskaming, see Richard Tatley, *Northern Steamboats: Temiskaming, Nipissing and Abitibi* (Erin, Ontario: Boston Mills Press, 1996) 69-70; 95.

8.   In 1811, a new store and some other buildings were erected to replace the original fort established on the east shore of the lake at the Narrows in 1688. This configuration of Fort Temiskamingue was referred to as the "Old Fort." By 1869, buildings dating from 1811 were

used as wholesale warehouses open only to HBC employees, while the new buildings constructed that year were utilized for retail transactions. George L. Cassidy, *Arrow North*, 71.

9.   The upper Quebec shore of Lake Temiskaming would have been the territory of Temiskaming band of the Algonquins, although there was likely some intermingling with the Ojibwa Temagami band from the western side of the lake. Cassidy, *Arrow North*, 30.

10.   The language used here reflects the ethnic and cultural biases of the time. While the term is derived from an aboriginal word meaning younger woman, its use by Europeans in reference to aboriginal women is derogatory.

11.   Mr. Coster could have been an acquaintance expected to arrive on the *Argo*. Piche, as A.H. Telfer recounted, was originally from the Quebec side of the lake, maintaining farms on both sides, and a rudimentary sawmill at the mouth of Mill Creek. It would seem that he often provided assistance and company to Temiskaming travellers. In George L. Cassidy's local history, a John Piche is identified as one of a group of men who formed the Temiskaming and Hudson Bay (mining) Company which successfully staked claims in the Cobalt silver boom. Cassidy, *Arrow North*, 145. See also the following excerpt on Edouard Piche by Bruce W. Taylor:

Edouard Piche

One of the earliest settlers and one of the most colourful characters of the Lake Temiskaming area was Edouard Piche. Born in 1820 at Allumette Island on the Ottawa River, Piche arrived at Lake Temiskaming in the winter of 1862-63 to cut timber for Thomas Murray of Pembroke, who with his brother, William Murray had been active in trading along the Ottawa River and up the Dumoine River.[1] (*Daniel Côté and Comité du livre de St-Bruno-de-Guigues, Regarde, j'ai tant à te dire. Saint-Bruno-de-Guiges, Quebec: Comité du livre de St-Bruno-De-Guigues 1997.*)

In the fall of 1863, Piche located on Lot 20, concession 1, of Guigues Township and established a fur trading business. This location happened to be part of a beaver meadow where the Hudson's Bay Company was accustomed to pasture its cattle and where marsh hay was cut. Piche invoked the displeasure of the company officials, when by offering whisky and higher prices for furs, he was able to divert away from the company some members of the Abitibi Natives who brought him any furs they had left over after pay their debts to the company. Hamilton, the Chief Factor at Fort Temiskaming, sent two of the company's employees to build a house beside Piche and to clear land. This establishment, called "Fort Roth," and the resultant close surveillance of Piche soon put him out of business. In 1864, Piche moved his store a short distance away to Lot 14, concession 1, Guigues Township, where he continued to farm and trade as an agent of Thomas Murray. This location, which included a point which ran into the lake, was later called "Point Piche."[2] *(Elaine Mitchell,* Fort Temiskaming and the Fur Trade. *Toronto: University of Toronto Press, 1977.)* Thomas Murray later settled at North Temiskaming (or Tête du Lac), which later became known as Notre Dame du Nord, and attempted to have a subdivision of the town named "Murray City," but the locals, a mixture of French Canadians and Algonquin Natives objected, and the name did not stand. Murray later became a member of the provincial legislature for Renfrew County in Ontario, and also a member of the National Assembly of Quebec for Pontiac County.[3] *(Augustin Chénier,* Notes Historiques Sur le Témiscamingue. *Ville Marie, Quebec: 1937.)*

Edouard Piche's wife, Marguerite McAdam, was born in Ireland. The had seven children, some of whom became well known in the district. The children were: Flore and Suzanne (both of whom became nuns); Eliza (also known as Elizabeth), the wife of Indian Agent, Adam Burwash; Annie (wife of Alfred Morin); John (or Jean) Joseph; and Thomas (who married Flaviene Berthoaume). Thanks to his success in business, Piche was able to provide an education for all four of his daughters.

Recognizing the need for a gristmill to service the growing number of farms in the area, Edouard Piche and his sons obtained a government permit to build a gristmill at Mill Creek, a small fast-flowing creek on the Ontario shore of the lake.[4] *(Marc Riopel, Sur les traces des Robes Noires. Ville Marie, Quebec: Société d'histoire du Témiscamingue, undated.)* The date of the establishment of the mill is in question. Some publications give the date as 1874, while others place it at 1879. Archival research indicates that in October 1877, the Chief of the North Temiskaming band, Massinigijik, petitioned the Department of Indian Affairs for a gristmill. He was supported by Rev. Father J.M. Pian, a priest at the Mission Saint Claude. The mill was to be built at Mill Creek, one of the few creeks with the fall of water necessary to run the mill. Funding was approved by Indian Affairs by February 1879, and the mill was completed and operational by July 1879. A report by the inspector of Indian Agencies and reserves dated November 21, 1883 the following:

21 November 1883: Report to L. Vankoughnet, Deputy Supt General of Indian Affairs from S. Dingman, Inspector of Indian Agencies & Reserves, Ottawa (NA RG10 Vol. 7625 File 17,035-1 Reel C-11,584 - Timiskaming Agency – Correspondence regarding mills in general (1877-1927) :

On the 10th I visited the grist mill built by the late Joseph Piche under an agreement entered into between him and the Rev Jean Marie Pian of the Temiscamingue Indian Mission on the 15th of February 1879. Towards the construction of this mill the Department contributed liberally in view of the advantages it was supposed it would afford to the Indians on the Temiscamingue Reserve. it is situated on the Ontario side of the Lake, about 14 miles below the Reserve, and in passing by canoe or boat between it and the Reserve a large bay had to be crossed, and in general the course is much exposed and in high winds the passage would be dangerous, if not impracticable. At the mill the shore is much exposed to south, east and north winds. I found the mill built upon a very rapid stream, called Mill Creek, about one eighth of a mile from the lake. The banks are very high, fully 100 feet or more at the mill, and render the construction of a dam very easy, and without the least flooding of land. The same is built about 50 or 60 feet above the mill, with a reserve dam about half or three quarters of a mile further up the stream, and the aggregate water fall from the reserve dam to the Lake must be 100 or 150 feet at least. The road from the mill to the Lake is quite precipitous, but has been considerably excavated, and it is quite practicable to take a small load on a cart up or down it. I found the mill as far as I could judge, apparently in fair running order; the water wheel, stones and gold all seemed to be in good order. [Previous sentence underlined by subsequent reader.] The Stones were said to have been used one year before they were placed in this mill. See the other machinery I should think had been placed new in the mill. There was a new smut machine in the mill but it had not been set up ready for being operated.

John Piche who is now in possession of the mill showed me all the necessary tools for making any ordinary repairs, which he always kept conveniently on hand. I should think the cost of the construction of the dams and the mill, with the machinery, would fully equal the original estimated cost of $900 or $1000. There is a saw mill attached, but it is not yet enclosed.

John Piche, the present reputed owner, has recently been married, and resides at the mill, and has a clearing of 5 or 6 acres, adjoining the mill. He keeps a horse and cart to haul the grists to and from the mill from the lake. His ownership to the mill will be shown by the article of agreement between the late Joseph Piche and the Rev Jean Marie Pian, dated 15th February 1879, and the article of an agreement between the late Joseph Piche and the same John Piche, dated 3rd March 1879, a duplicate of which I append to this report.

The mill site is not deeded land, but the title is yet in the Crown, and I could not learn whether it had been located to the Piches. I would beg to suggest that it would be perhaps well for the Department to inquire of the Ontario Government what claims the Piches have to the site before any further advances are made. Neither is the mill insured. John Piche said he could not get it insured as it was in unorganized territory. I would beg to suggest, also, the propriety of making inquiry as to whether it can be insured or not, and if it can, to effect an insurance.

Piche says that $293.81 advanced by the Department was duly paid over by the Rev. Jean Marie Pian to his late brother Joseph Piche, to aid in the erection of the mill, but the $300 surplus funds of the Ontario Government was not paid over, except the value of about two barrels of pork. But the Rev. Father Deleage says he has been informed that it was duly paid over, and that receipts can be shown.

The only difficulty in the way of running the mill, that I could see, whenever there is grain to grind, is the ability of the present owner, John Piche, to run it. He claims, however, that he can run it and make good flour, that he has now had two year experience in milling and for a time, was engaged in one of the best mills in Toronto, and worked specially at dressing stones with the view to qualifying himself to run his mill on the Temiscamingue. He is willing to bind himself to carry out the conditions in which the Department agreed to assist in the construction of the mill, and named, as his sureties, John Poupore Esq., Crown Land Agent Quebec, Ottawa, and WJ Poupore, MPP for Pontiac, Quebec.

The Joseph Piche mentioned above as the builder of the mill died in Mattawa on April 4, 1910. [5] (Pembroke Observer, *April 16, 1880.*)

Edouard Piche retired in 1901, and sold his land in Guigues Township. He moved with his wife to Ville Marie and later to Nôtre Dame du Nord where he died on October 2, 1903. His wife, Marguerite McAdam died two years later in 1905. They are buried together in the Nôtre Dame du Nord Cemetery.

Elizabeth Piche, who married Adam Burwash on September 3, 1888, (Pembroke Observer, *September 21, 1888*) became well known as a champion of the rights of the Natives in Abitibi-Temiskaming. She was born on Allumette Island in 1862. Adam Burwash, who was born at Lachute, Quebec, in 1850, worked on survey parties in the north, as early as 1870, and in 1873 took up land on the edge of the Native reserve near present-day Nôtre Dame du Nord. He served as Indian Agent for eleven years and also as a magistrate and councillor in the town of Ville Marie. In 1903, Burwash became involved as a director of the famous Temiskaming and Hudson Bay Mining Company, with headquarters in New Liskeard. His wife Elizabeth was instrumental in having the Lady Minto Hospital built at New Liskeard. The Burwash family later moved to a farm near Earlton, where they were burnt out in the great fire of 1922. She wrote a letter to Lady Minto, wife of the Governor General of Canada asking for her support, and was successful in receiving the vice-regal patronage and a donation of $2000. The hospital was the first built north of North Bay, in 1907. The family moved to Noranda, Quebec, in 1927. Adam Burwash died at Noranda in 1937; his wife died 10 years later.

John (Jean) Piche, who took over the operation of the gristmill at Mill Creek from his deceased brother, Joseph, lead an interesting life. He was retained as a prospector by the consortium of New Liskeard investors who organized the famous Temiskaming and Hudson Bay Mining Company in 1902, and played a leading role in developing a rich silver mine at Cobalt, early in the life of that mining camp. He later gained some notoriety when he disappeared and was declared a fugitive following an investigation into the affairs of the company. He was later acquitted of any wrongdoing.

12. Cassidy, *Arrow North*, 350.

13. This deep creek was probably an intersection with the meandering course of Mill Creek.

14. Charles Cobbald Farr, originally from England, had been in the employ of the Hudson's Bay Company since 1878, having served as factor at Fort Kipawa from that time until his promotion to Fort Temiskamingue in 1882. His colourful life and tireless crusade on

behalf of northern development are recounted by Peter Fancy in *Temiskaming Treasure Trails 1886-1903* (Cobalt, Ontario: Highway Book Shop, 1992).

15.   Fancy, *Temiskaming Treasure Trails 1886-1903*, 29-30.

16.   The Matabanick Portage, an original route of Native Peoples and traders, left the shore of Lake Temiskaming at Humphrey's Depot. When C.C. Farr's general store was granted a post office, Farr chose to name it after his old school, Haileybury, in England. The name Matabanick was given to a hotel in the new settlement. Vestiges of the name can still be seen on the side of a wooden building. Fancy, *Temiskaming Treasure Trails*, 27.

17.   However understated, injuries sustained in the bush could have serious consequences. Such were the harsh realities of working on the survey, especially for the newcomer.

18.   Niven in his field notes refers to this terrain as "*brûlé*," the French term for land recently ravaged by forest fire. "Field Notes of Outlines of Townships at the Head of Lake Temiscamingue 1886," 8.

19.   Abandoning earlier practice of establishing boundaries by following natural features of watercourses and hills, Niven outlined his townships exactly six miles square (Bucke being the exception; the missing northeast chunk was claimed on Wahbe's Point). Running north each mile was noted. Other surveyors would follow later, dividing the townships into six east-west concessions numbered from south to north, then subdividing each concession into twelve north-south lots, each one mile long by half mile wide. See *Temiskaming Treasure Trails*, 11; and *Ontario Surveys and the Land Surveyor*, 187.

20.   Noting the same spectacular view, Niven talks of "a smoky line indicating the Blanche River." This would have been seven to eight miles cross country, from their situation near the northwest corner of

Township 1 (Bucke)."Field Notes,"'E.' A series of rocky ridges ran north-westerly into the unsurveyed land later to be designated as Hudson Township. Large areas of slate and visible outcroppings of limestone resembling the Niagara Escarpment formation were described in a later Crown Lands Department publication, *Northern Districts of Ontario, Canada, 1895* (Toronto:Warwick Bros. & Rutter, 1895) 62.

21.   In his field notes for August 8, Niven remarks, "Continued line east. Telfer laid up with cut leg." Obviously the injury sustained on July 13 was more serious than reported, and was aggravated by daily work. "Field Notes," 10.

22.   See additional the following material on early white settlers and Edouard Piche from Bruce W. Taylor, *New Liskeard: The Pioneer Years* (Cobalt, Ontario: Highway Book Shop, 2003):

The Settlers

"The first permanent white settlers on Lake Temiskaming were retired lumbermen who took advantage of opportunities to supply the lumber camps with fresh produce, and hay for the thousands of horses that were used to skid the logs to the lakes. Marsh hay was a native grass that grew commonly on the flat areas around the north end of the lake, and was harvested by settlers (or squatters, since they did not own their farms) for the lumber camps. Probably the first true settlers were ex-lumbermen Joseph Bonin and one Jolicoeur, who established small farms at the mouth of the Montreal River in the early 1850s. This particular site, where the Montreal River and the Matabitchewan River empty into Lake Temiskaming later became a busy depot for lumbermen and, later still, a small community attracted to the nearby silver mines of South Lorraine Township.

Edouard Piche came to Lake Temiskaming in 1862 to work in the timber trade for Thomas Murray of Pembroke. In 1863, Piche set himself up as an independent fur trader, and built a home about a kilometre north of Point Piche. By offering whisky and higher prices for furs than the Hudson's Bay Company, he was able to make inroads into the company's trade that could not be ignored. Subsequently, the HBC established an outpost, called Fort Wrath right beside Piche's post, eventually putting him out of business. Piche was forced to move and started a farm at Point Piche, where he acted as an agent for the Murray interests in the area. He obtained permission from the government in 1874 to build a gristmill, which was the first and only mill on the lake for many years. The grain grown by the Oblates at the Old Mission was milled at Piche's mill.

It was the Roman Catholic Church that first recognized the potential for agriculture in the Lake Temiskaming area, and also the potential for solving what was for them becoming a problem in southern Quebec. The Church was concerned that many French Canadians were migrating to the northeastern United States in search of jobs and land, and were losing their language and heritage. It saw the area as offering an alternative to the USA, and began encouraging settlement as early as 1882, when the first official colonists arrived.

In 1884, with the active participation of the Church, La Société de Colonization du Lac Témiscamingue was established with the goal of colonizing the northeast (Quebec) side of the lake, particularly the townships of Duhamel and Guigues. The barriers to transportation on the Upper Ottawa between Mattawa and Lake Temiskaming were addressed by making improvements to the five portages; specifically placing small steamboats between the rapids, and constructing narrow gauge railways around them. In 1885, there were 37 families located on farms; in 1886, 69 families; and by 1887, 92 families, with about 2,200 acres of land under cultivation.

By comparison, the townships on the Ontario side of the lake were not even surveyed until 1887 and, apart from C.C. Farr's settlement at Haileybury, which started in 1889, the first large-scale settlement of the Little Clay Belt did not start until 1894.

This, then sets the scene for the settlement of what later would become the town of New Liskeard, and the opening up of the fertile townships of Temiskaming's Little Clay Belt.

Excerpt from *Place Names of Temiskaming* by Bruce Taylor (New Liskeard, Ontario: White Mountain Publications, 2000).

Matabitchewan

"Matabitchewan (or Meydabeejeewan) is an Algonkian Native term meaning "where two rivers come together," and refers to the place where the Matabitchewan and Montreal rivers empty into Lake Temiskaming approximately 35 km south of Haileybury. This was one of the first areas in Temiskaming to be settled. In the 1860s, two ex-lumbermen from Beauharnois, Quebec, Jolicoeur and Bonin, established farms on the flat land where the Montreal and Matabitchewan rivers flow, a short distance apart, into Lake Temiskaming. By the turn of the century, other settlers, including several Scandinavian families had settled in this area. Some of the large lumber companies established farms at Matabitchewan where they kept horses during the summer months, and grew hay and vegetables for the lumber camps.

Following the development of the silver mines at Cobalt, a large hydroelectric plant was built on the Matabitchewan River in 1909-10. The dam was equipped with a log slide to enable the lumbermen to send logs over the dam into Lake Temiskaming. The plant was operated by the British Canadian Power Company, until acquired by the Northern Ontario Light and Power Company in 1912. It was later acquired by Ontario Hydro. The area was known as "Montreal River" in the 1901 census, but following the construction of a large hydroelectric plant in 1959, it became known as Matabitchewan. A post office was established at Montreal River as early as 1885, and operated until 1960. Daniel Jonason was the postmaster in 1919.

23. Niven had left some of his party with Charles F. Aylsworth, to whom he had also given responsibility for some of the survey between townships two and seven. He had then made his way four miles down the lake to Piche's farm to pick up Telfer, now recuperated. The group then returned to rendezvous with Aylsworth's party at the mouth of Wabi Creek.

24. In 1883, Edward Wright, an Ottawa businessman, began working a silver mine north of Baie-des-Pères, known as the Wright Mine. It was a fairly rich deposit of lead and silver-bearing galena, a lead ore. By 1885 it was yielding 10 tons of ore. At one point, the main shaft reached 250 feet with four levels. Over the next ten years the mine changed hands several times, always hampered, according to the operators, by lack of efficient transportation. Fancy, *Temiskaming Treasure Trails*, 113.

25. A.H. Telfer was probably using a phonetic spelling for land formerly held by a local Anishnawbe chief called Wabis, or Wabi. The chief's family eventually moved to the reserve at the head of the lake, but their name remained with the area. Tatley, *Northern Steamboats: Timiskaming, Nipissing & Abitibi*, 88. See also the following excerpt from Bruce W. Taylor, *New Liskeard: The Pioneer Years*, Chapter 2:

The Wabie Family at New Liskeard

"Nancy Wabie was a very determined lady. So determined, in fact, to get some compensation for the Wabie family lands she claimed were unfairly taken away, that over a 17 year period from 1917 to 1934, she carried on a spirited correspondence with various officials in Ottawa and Toronto, and even at one point wrote the Prime Minister, Sir Robert Borden, and threatened to go to Ottawa to confront him.[1] *(Letter from Nancy Wabie to Sir Robert Borden, March 13, 1918. In her letter to the Prime Minister, she wrote, "I will be down to Ottawa to see you this month to tell you all my trouble about this northland.")*
At the heart of the matter was Nancy Wabie's contention that her father, Joachim (also known as "Swishaw") Wabie[2] *(The spelling "Wabie" is used here as it appears to be the spelling of choice of the family. There have been several spellings used in various accounts in the past, including Wabi, Wahbi, and Wahbbi. The spelling "Wabi" is used to describe the Wabi River and Wabi Bay at New Liskeard)* had cleared land, and lived for fifty years on that land on the north side of the Wabi River, where the town of New Liskeard now stands. She claimed that the entire area around New Liskeard was part of the Wabie family's

traditional hunting territory for generations, that her father, was not associated with the North Temiskaming Band of natives, and that he had apparently been promised a payment of fifteen thousand dollars for his land-money which he did not receive.

Nancy Wabie never did get what she wanted, but her fight against the authorities is interesting in that it raises several questions that even now may never be answered fully. Could Joachim Wabie, of the well-know Wabigijic family, unilaterally divorce himself from the North Temiskaming Band in order to get compensation for land in Ontario? Was his occupation of the land at the mouth of the Wabi River considered a "permanent" occupation? Was there actually a verbal agreement between Joachim Wabi and the local Indian Agent regarding compensation? Did Nancy Wabie have a legitimate claim for compensation for her father's land after his death when her brothers and a sister accepted status as members of the North Temiskaming Band, and lived on reserve lands?

All of these questions provide an intriguing look at the history and geography of the land on the Ontario side of Lake Temiskaming that eventually became the town of New Liskeard.

The Wabigijic family is well known as being one of the leading families or clans of the North Temiskaming Band of the Algonkin group. Wabigijic in the Algonkian language means "White Sky," or "Sky without Clouds," and the totem that is emblematic of this family is the Caribou. The government anthropologist Speck[3] (F.G. Speck, Family Hunting Territories and Social Life of Various Algonkian Bands of the Ottawa Valley. Canada Department of Mines, Memoir 70, No. 8, Anthropological Series, 1915) noted that the Wabigijic family was one of "... seven original constituents of the Temiskaming band, so far as is now known. Some have about lost their identity through intermarriage with outsiders."

Joachim Wabigijic

Early records of the Hudson's Bay Company and the Oblate missionaries generally identified the Natives with whom they were dealing only by last name, and it is difficult to distinguish between them. In addition, the European concept of a family or Christian name did not come into general usage until the mid-1800s, and there is a period of overlap, when both the old Algonkian and the new Christian names were used. The government surveyors, O'Hanly and O'Dwyer in their 1873 report mention "... an Indian settler, Wabigijic, on a point named after him." That point is now known as Dawson Point, on Lake Temiskaming east of New Liskeard. Father Paradis' 1882 map of Lake Temiskaming shows a "ferme de Wabigijic" located on this same point, but no indication of a farm at the mouth of the Wabi River.

Joachim Wabigijic, after whom New Liskeard's Wabi River is named, was the son of a Native trapper named Kijiko8inini,[4] *(The Oblate priests, in recording the names of Natives used an "8" in the spelling of the name to refer to the sound "huit" (eight in French)* and his wife Oticpikijikokwe. They were recorded as trading at the Fort in the period 1816-1827. Both were born before 1790, and died before their son Joachim was married in 1845. Joachim was born about 1816, and on June 17, 1845, married Angelique (Angèle) Ob8itasinoki8e (Lapointe). Father Laverlochère, the Oblate priest who performed the marriage noted that Angèle was the daughter of Marie Louise 8ijikaba8ite, the "country wife" of one Lapointe. Angèle's mother was not alive at the time of the marriage and, because she was a minor (probably about 15 years old), she had the permission of her grandmother to marry.

When the Roman Catholic Bishop Duhamel made a visit to Temiskaming in 1881, Joachim and Jean Wabigijic were identified as paddlers in one of the two canoes that carried the Bishop and his entourage on his trip from Lake Temiskaming to Father Nedelec's mission at Lake Abitibi.[5] *(Augustin Chénier,* Notes Historiques sur le Temiscamingue, *Ville Marie: 1937).* The relationship between the two Wabigijics is not known, and in fact Joachim and Jean could be father and son, or brothers, the sons of Joachim. In any case, Joachim Wabigijic, the elder, who in 1881 would have been 65 years old, was a well-known resident of Lake Temiskaming and enjoyed some repute as a paddler.

It was this Joachim Wabigijic, known by the nickname "Swishaw,"[6] *(The large hydroelectric dam on the Ottawa River near Deep River in Renfrew County is called the Des Joachim Dam, and is known locally as the "Swishaw" Dam)* who made a small clearing at the mouth of the

Wabi River, erected a cabin there, and apparently lived there for some 50 years. The Wabigijic patronymic was unwieldy for the first white men, and was shortened to Wabi (or Wabie). (Frank Wabie told me the reason it was shortened was that the white man couldn't spell Wabigijic!)[7] *(Interview by author Bruce W. Taylor with Frank Wabie, North Temiskaming Reserve, September 19, 1991. I have used the spelling "Wabigijic," which appears to be the preferred spelling, except where it is spelled differently in quotes.)*

Joachim Wabigijic was born in the Lake Temiskaming area, and apparently spent most of his life there. In 1849, the Oblate Missionaries asked the federal government to establish a reserve at the head of Lake Temiskaming at "Tête du lac," or North Temiskaming, for the local Algonquins. The reserve, created in 1851, initially contained 230,000 acres, but it gradually was decreased to its present much-diminished size. As a member of the Temiskaming Band of the Algonkin group, Wabigijic would have been included in the band when the Robinson Treaty of 1849 went into effect. The natives of the Temiskaming band at this time were migratory, spending most of the year (September through May) on their trap lines and hunting grounds, and summering at the small village at Tête du lac.

Joachim Wabigijic and his wife Angèle Lapointe, had seven known children, all of whom are known by the name Wabie. They were Angèle (Katt) (1839-1926), John (1856-1929), Angus (1858-?), Annie (1860-?), William, Nancy (1862-) and Joachim (1864-?). Nancy Wabie states that her father lived for fifty years at his place on the Wabi River, and that she was born there in 1862. If that was the case, the other children of Joachim and Angèle Wabigijic probably were also born at that place.

Madeline Katt Theriault, a great-granddaughter of Angèle Wabie, states in her book *Moose to Moccasins: The Story of Ka Kita Wa Pa No Kwe*[8] (Toronto: Natural Heritage, 1992) that her great-grandmother's parents, Joachim and Angèle Wabigijic, had 16 children, and they were "... the first ones to make a clearing at a river now called Wabie River. The river was named after them. The Wabies lived there until the white man came to New Liskeard and pushed them off their land. They lost their homes and moved to North Temiskaming to an Indian village there, but they never got a thing for their land – not one cent."

Historically, the chiefs of the Temiskaming Band were derived from the Massinagijik family, who were the hereditary bearers of this honour. When Chief Hillarion Massinagijic died during the winter of 1881-1882, a gathering of the families at the Mission St. Claude declared his son Solomon Massinagijic the new chief, and Angus Wabigijic was elected Assistant Chief. It is unlikely that previous generations of Wabigijics had been baptized. Father Mourier states, in the "Codex Historicus" of the Oblate Fathers, that the ancestors of Hillarion Massinagijik were *"infidèles et payens,"* thus it is likely that the generation of Joachim Wabigijic and Hillarion Massinagijik were the first of their families to be converted.[9] *(Marc Riopel,* Sur les traces des Robes Noires. *Ville Marie, Quebec: Société d'Histoire du Témiscamingue, undated.)* There is no record of when Joachim Wabigijic was converted to the Christian faith; however, as a contemporary of Hillarion Massinagijik (1817-1862), who had been converted,[10] *(Father Martineau, in his history of the Old Mission,* Document Historique No.1-La Veille Mission, *1989, states that the date of Massinagijik's conversion was not known, but in 1860 he was one of the signatories to a request to have a permanent missionary sent to Temiskaming.)* and because he had been married in the Roman Catholic Church, it is likely that he also had been baptized.

On the question of the traditional hunting rights to the area around New Liskeard, there can be no argument. For generations the area that now includes the towns of New Liskeard and Haileybury (and possibly Cobalt) had been part of the hunting territory of the Wabigijic family or clan. F.G. Speck, in his 1915 memoir states:

"The matter, however, which constitutes the main bond of union and interest in these (family) groups is the family hunting territory, in which all male members share the right of hunting and fishing. These hunting 'lots' or territories are more or less fixed tracts of country whose boundaries are determined by certain rivers, ridges, lakes, or other natural landmarks, such as swamps and clumps of cedars or pines. Hunting outside of one's inherited territory was punishable occasionally by death."

The Wabigijic family's hunting territory, which Speck outlined on a map, encompassed the area northwest of Lake Temiskaming, including the basin of Wabi Creek. The eastern boundary of the territory was at Sutton Bay, on Lake Temiskaming, and extended northward, parallel to the Blanche River to approximately present-day Belle Vallée, then curved west and south to encompass the upper reaches of the Wabi River (approximately at Milberta), and swung south to encompass the west branch of the Wabi, then east to the shore of Lake Temiskaming near Haileybury. Speck shows a narrow strip of land along the west shore of the lake from Haileybury to the Montreal River as being part of this territory.

The Wabigijic territory was bounded to the south by the Massinagijik territory – south and west of the Montreal River, to the west by the Kitcibien and Cabedia territories, and on the east by the Wadewesis territory extending into Quebec along the Quinze River.

When Joachim Wabigijic died in 1888, there were no white settlers yet established on the Wabi River. The Townships of Dymond (in which New Liskeard lies), and Harris (containing Dawson Point), had only been surveyed the previous year (1887). George Dawson arrived on the shore of Wabi (later Dawson) Point in 1888, and apparently purchased a farm from the Wabie family. Unfortunately, there is no record of how much was paid for the farm, or to whom the payment was made. Presumably Dawson acquired it from one of Joachim Wabigijic's sons.

The Children of Joachim Wabigijic and Angèle Lapointe

Joachim Wabigijic and Angèle Lapointe had ten known children. The following is a brief description of six of these, including some who were well-known in the New Liskeard area. Charles and William Wabie were born in 1851 and 1852 respectively, but they, and a younger brother,

Noel, born in 1866, are not listed on the 1871 census, and may have died young or left the area.

Angèle Wabie

Angèle Wabie is best known as the revered grandmother of Madeline Katt Theriault, author of a fascinating book on her (Madeline's) life entitled *Moose to Moccasins: The Story of Ka Kita Wa Pa No Kwe.* Angèle, who Madeline Katt Theriault calls her "Great-Grandmother," was the one who raised young Madeline when her mother died, and taught her many of the old customs. Madeline says of her Grandmother: "My Great-grandmother was married from the Wabie River. As her husband, Michel Katt, was a man from Bear Island they made their home there. For hunting grounds they trapped at Maple Mountain and all through Florence Lake and McPherson Lake."[11] *(Theriault,* Moose to Moccasins, *1992.)*

Madeline states that Angèle Katt had fifteen children, including twin girls (who both drowned at age twenty-five), and that she died at Bear Island in March 1926, at the age of eighty-seven. These statistics would place her birth year at 1839, which means that either Madeline's estimate of her grandmother's age at death was in error, or the birth year of Angèle Lapointe, Angèle's mother (1830) is in error, since it would make her nine years old when Angèle was born. The 1901 census for the Montreal River (between Gillies Limit and Matachewan) lists a Machelle Cat, hunter and trapper (born in Ontario, September 26, 1845) and his wife, Angelline (born in Ontario, August 1, 1850). Three children are also listed: Terrance (born 1880), Mathew (born 1882) and Augustus (born 1890). There are several Cat families listed for Lake Temagami, but no Angèle or Angelline. Thus, if this data is correct, Angèle Wabie was the oldest known child of Joachim Wabigijic and his wife, born in 1850.

One of the fifteen children of Angèle and Michel Katt was Elizabeth Petrant, Madeline Katt Theriault's mother, who died in 1922 after delivering twins. Madeline Theriault herself was born on September 8, 1908, and spent her latter years in North Bay and is now deceased.

John Wabie

John Wabie was born in 1856, probably at the Wabigijic home at the Wabi River. His sister, Nancy Wabie, who provides the most detailed account of the family, indicates that her brothers (John included), married women from the North Temiskaming Reserve, and moved there, becoming members of that band. There is some confusion about the date that happened. Nancy Wabie states that she was left alone at age 16 (1878) when her mother died; however, her mother did not die until May 4, 1895. It is likely that the family moved to North Temiskaming after Joachim's death in 1888. John Wabie married Eliza Stanger and had eight children, the oldest of whom was born in 1886, and the youngest in 1902.

Angus Wabie

Perhaps the best known of Joachim's sons was Angus Wabie, usually called "Chief" Wabie. The earliest mention of him was the description of the election of a new Chief of the Band in 1882, when he was declared Assistant Chief. There is no indication that he was actually elected Chief of the Band, and the "Assistant" appellation may have led to his being called "Chief" by the white settlers.

Angus Wabie was mentioned in the memoirs of C.C. Farr, the founder of the town of Haileybury, as early as 1889. Farr had resigned his position with the Hudson's Bay Company, and taken up a plot of land at Humphry's Landing at the Lake Temiskaming terminus of the age-old Matabanik trail to the Montreal River. In 1889, he constructed a house there, and Angus Wabie had a contract to supply the timbers.[12] *(C.C. Farr, The Life of Charles Cobold Farr, Founder of the Town of Haileybury, District of Temiskaming, Ontario. Privately published by the granddaughters of C.C. Farr, 1967.)* Anson Gard, an American who wrote a book about the Temiskaming District also mentions Angus Wabie is a somewhat condescending manner, with a description of how Wabie dealt with the white man in the sale of some hay during a time when that commodity was scarce in the north.[13] *(Anson Gard, North Bay, The Gateway to Silverland. Toronto: The Emerson Press, 1909.)*

Angus Wabie was a frequent visitor to New Liskeard, and was well-known to the earliest settlers. Most commented on the fact that Wabie was able to adapt quite well to the encroachment of civilization, and was accepted on equal terms by those who had dealings with him. He was also one of the first Natives (and one of the first in the area) to own an automobile.

One of New Liskeard's pioneer industries was the Wabi Iron Works. Hugh A. McEwan, who co-founded the foundry in 1907, explains the origin of the firm's name as follows:

"Why the name Wabi? The name was chosen first because of its brevity, and second because it was the name of an Indian Chief whose camp was at the mouth of the river where McCamus and McKelvie mills were located. Chief Wabi had a reputation for strength and honesty and the "Wabi" company maintained these characteristics."[14] *(H.A. McEwan,* A Brief History of the Wabi Iron Works Limited. *New Liskeard Ontario: unpublished, 1945.)*

McEwan had a curiosity about the Wabie family, and apparently conducted some research into their history. In a letter to W.S. Carr, manager of the foundry in 1945, he stated:

"As a sideline, I used to get all the information possible regarding Chief Wabi and his family. I used to have a photo of his boys. Mr. Bell, of Mattawa, who was a Dominion Government representative, got the two boys, John and Justice,[15] *(There is no record of a son named "Justice." Mr. McEwan may have confused that name with the name of Angus Wabie's son August, or Augustus. Also, there is no record of a son John. Angus Wabie's sons were named James, August, Benjamin and Joseph. Three daughters were named Theresa, Agnes and Rose Anna.)* to make a trip to the Yukon when the gold rush was on, and report what they thought of the country.

Mr. Bell informed the writer that when they returned after being gone about a year, they came into his store and when asked what kind of a trip they had, had no information to give. This lot of Indians were a very quiet crowd and did very little talking. I was told by another party that you could be with them for a whole day, and hardly a word would be spoken."[16] *(H.A. McEwan, Letter to W.S. Carr, July 31, 1945.)*

Unfortunately, Mr. McEwan's notes on his research into the Wabie family have not yet come to light.

Angus Wabie was born in 1856, probably at the Wabi River. He was married twice; the first time to Marie Thivierge (date unknown). Their children were James, August, Theresa, Joseph, Benjamin, Agnes, and Rose Anna. After the death of his first wife, he remarried in January 30, 1905, at Notre Dame du Nord, to Jane Moar, the widow of Joseph Frank. His name was entered in the registry as Angus "Wabikijik."

Annie Wabie

Annie Wabie was born in 1860, probably at the Wabi River location. She married John George McBride, who became Chief of the North Temiskaming Band. They had two sons, Ernest (Molush) McBride, and Hector McBride, and one daughter, Delphine McBride, who apparently married into the Katt family from Bear Island.

Joachim Wabie

The youngest of the children of Joachim Wabigijic and Angèle Lapointe appears to be Joachim Wabie, born about 1864. Also known by the nickname "Washaw," Joachim was married twice – first to Betsi Chromate, with whom he had four children, and second, on August 13, 1901 (at North Temiskaming), to Therese Razo.[17] *(Most of the actual dates for marriages in this family are from a published source entitled "Repertoire des Marriages du Comte de Temiscamingue." This publication was accessed in the North Bay Public Library.)* There were no children from the second marriage.

Barney Wabie was the best known of Joachim and Betsi's children, and even better known was Barney's son, Frank Wabie, who died on June 11, 1993, at the age of 92. In a interview taped on September 19, 1991, Frank Wabie indicated that when he was a youngster, his family used to spend the winters on the Ontario side of Lake Temiskaming, near the site of the present-day Rexwood particle board plant, located approximately half-way between Haileybury and New Liskeard.

Although he was born at North Temiskaming, Frank Wabie indicated that from the time he was born in 1900 until 1911 (when the family moved to Kenogami, near Kirkland Lake), his family spent the summers at North Temiskaming, and the winters in Ontario ....

Frank's mother, Mary Ann Miness, was the daughter of Angus Miness, known as "Shawwanbi." Frank indicated that he had a brother Norman, and a sister, "Kittens," as well as two half-sisters (the daughters of Barney Wabie and Sophie Anderson), Bernadette and Nora.

In 1927, Frank married Annie Reynolds, and they had ten children, most of whom live at North Temiskaming, although some live as far away as Woodstock and Ignace, Ontario. Frank Wabie passed away on June 11, 1993, at the age of 92. He is buried in the Jawbones Bay Cemetery at Kipawa, Quebec. His obituary states that he left 52 grandchildren, 56 great-grandchildren, and 6 great-great-grandchildren.

Nancy Wabie

The woman who caused all the fuss from 1917 to 1934 with her demands for compensation for her father's land was Nancy Wabie, the youngest of the Wabigijic daughters. She was born in 1862 on the banks of the Wabi River, at a place that later became the town of New Liskeard. She never married.

The rationale for her case for compensation was that her family were not members of the North Temiskaming Band and, consequently, did not surrender their traditional hunting lands, and particularly the land at the mouth of the Wabi River on which the family lived, and on which, according to Nancy, her father Joachim Wabigijic lived for fifty years. Also, she claims that her father was promised a payment of fifteen thousand dollars for the land by the Indian Agent, a Mr. Harry Woods.

The correspondence over seventeen years in this case includes 19 letters and memos – some handwritten by Nancy Wabie, others by lawyers retained by her, and the rest from various provincial and federal government officials.

In Nancy Wabie's first letter, dated July 6, 1917, and addressed to the Secretary of the Department of Indian Affairs, the frustration is evident, and Miss Wabie covered a lot of grievances. The letter is as follows:

To: The Secretary, Department of Indian Affairs, Ottawa

Dear Sir:

I would like to know if I am going to get anything for our land that was sold in New Ontario in the property of New Liskeard which is a town now. And about my great-grandfather's hunting ground from Cobalt and Elk Lake and Swastika up to Timmins. All this was my father's hunting ground and now those white people are making all kinds of money in timber and mines. When they first come up, we use them the best we could. We are working for them the best we can and they don't pay us enough that why we never got anything ahead. We are getting poorer all the time. I cannot forget that you sold my land and I want you to understand me. Who was the first here in New Ontario – Indian or White man, and I am going to tell you the same thing I told you last summer. Those Rastoules from French River – their grandfather is from France and yet they get the Indian money. When did you ever see anything good from France. And now none of them try to help you and the Wabis are gone to help in the war. I often think of my grandfather when he was free of his own land. And I find as if I was in jail since twenty-five years, and I tried nearly all the lawyers up in this northern country to try and get something for that property in New Liskeard. It cost me about three hundred dollars now. I tryid Mr. George Cohban, the Indian Agent about ten years ago. I ask fifteen thousand dollars for the property in New Liskeard and they told me that the government took everything in New Ontario and if I should try to get it that I would get in jail.

My father died in November 15, 1888 and I buried it at North Temiskaming in the Indian Reserve and they charge me five dollars for the land just enough for my father and they change the cemetery and I had to move my father again and they charge me eight dollars for another piece of land. They don't even give us enough land to bury one another. That ought to give you an idea that I am not in the band of North Temiskaming. I don't understand this game laws that we cannot kill any beaver, otter, or moose or any other game until we pay the license which is a fee of $5.00. And I see the white people wearing beaver coats and otter caps and muffs. Is it only the Indians that you forbid to kill those animals. I don't see any Indians to wear any furs. I am betting lawyer McDougall of Haileybury to send you down the birth of my father and hope you will find it. I enclose there with 3 cent stamp to answer my letter.

Yours Obedient Servant
Miss Nancy Wabi
Timmins

I forgot to tell you that our father's name was Joachim Wabikijik and since the white people came they made it Wabi instead.

What followed, between the years 1917 and 1934, was an exchange of letters (seven of which appear to be in Nancy Wabie's own hand), in which the responsibility for determining the validity of Miss

Wabi's claim was passed from the Federal Department of Indian Affairs, to the Ontario Department of Lands and Forests, to the Prime Minister's Office, to Indian Agents in Sturgeon Falls, Ontario, and Notre Dame du Nord, Quebec. From a historical perspective, the most interesting letters are Nancy Wabie's first letter of July 6, 1917 (above), and the letter of July 11, 1917, from her Lawyer, J. Lorn McDougall, of Haileybury. Mr. McDougall's letter is as follows:

July 11, 1917

Deputy Minister of Indian Affairs
Ottawa, Ontario

I have been asked by Miss Nancy Wabie, whose Indian name is Nancy Wabikijik, to write to you in regard to some allowances for property of her fathers which was taken away from the family without any compensation to her.

The facts are set out in her declaration dated the 6th of July, declaration of Mrs. Burwash[18] *(Mrs. Burwash was the wife of the former Indian Agent at North Temiskaming, Adam Burwash. She was well known in the communities on both sides of Lake Temiskaming, as her father, Edouard Piche, was one of the first independent traders on Lake Temiskaming, arriving in 1854. Mrs. Burwash took an interest in the affairs of the Indians on the North Temiskaming Reserve, to the extent that she apparently attempted to intervene in later years when much of the Indian land was surrendered to settlers.)* the same date and the declaration of John George McBride[19] *(John George McBride was the Chief of the North Temiskaming Band at that time, and was married to Nancy Wabi's sister, Annie.)* of the same date. They are shortly as follows, -

Her father, Joachim Wabikijik, had made a clearing at the mouth of the Wabie River, now the site of the Town of New Liskeard, and when that was surveyed, the surveyor marked the clearing on the map, but the land was afterwards granted without any reference to the Indian title. It appeared that the father had died in the meantime, and that his son, John Wabikijik, made a bargain with a man named Harry Woods, an Indian Agent, to sell the property and received $10.00 from Woods. Woods told them, that is the family, that they would receive $15,000 for the property, but apparently he did not get anything or in some way let the matter go so that they received nothing.

It seems like a real hardship that the original settlers in a town like New Liskeard could not get some recognition, or at least that his family should not get something. Would it be possible to get her some recognition. I thought perhaps that they could be given land somewhere else.

I would be glad to know if anything can be done for this woman.

I enclose you herewith, in addition to the declaration, two certificates, one as to the marriage of her father and mother, and the other the certificate of registration of her birth.

Yours truly

J. Lorn McDougall

Nancy Wabie was obviously not a person who was intimidated by bureaucracy, and on March 13, 1918, while in Calydor Hospital in Gravenhurst, Ontario, she wrote directly to the Prime Minister, Sir Robert Borden. In her letter, she repeated her arguments about owner-ship of the land at the Wabi River, and in closing, included this promise: "I will be down to Ottawa to see you this month to tell you all my trouble about this northland."

No doubt the prospect of dealing with a very determined Indian lady made the Prime Minister (who had a nasty war and the conscription issue on his hands) somewhat nervous, and he lost no time in having his secretary forward a letter to A. Campbell Scott, Assistant Superintendent General, Department of Indian Affairs, advising him that "... nothing is to be gained by Miss Wabi coming to Ottawa," and asking the Deputy Superintendent General to deal with the matter.

By 1919, the issue appeared to have boiled down to a question of whether or not Joachim Wabigijik and his children were recognized as being members of the North Temiskaming Band. Nancy Wabie retained another lawyer, H.E. McKee of Elk Lake, who, in a letter of February 3, 1919, tried to convince the Department of Indian Affairs that Joachim Wabigijik was a part of the Turtle Lake Band, and his three sons, Joachim, John and Angus, married into the North Temiskaming Band and now belong there. For her part, Nancy Wabie was attempting to prove that she was not recognized as an Indian, and never accepted treaty money, and would therefore be eligible for payment for the land.

In February 1919, the Indian Agent at North Temiskaming, Mr. J.A. Renaud was instructed to submit a full report on the matter, which he did on March 28, 1919. In his reply, he states categorically that, "Her father, the late Joachim Wabie, was recognized as an Indian and member of the Temiskaming Band."

This was not to be the end of the matter, however, as the Department, in an apparent bid to buy her off, sent Nancy Wabie a bizarre letter, along with a cheque for $2.91. The letter, from the Assistant Deputy and Secretary, and (perhaps appropriately) dated April 1, 1919, stated:

> I beg to transmit herewith cheque No. 83 for $2.91 in your favor being arrears of interest money due you as a member of the Temiscamingue Band. As this band does not participate in the payment of Robinson Treaty annuity, you are not entitled to receive payment of annuity.

Whoever had decided to take this approach with Nancy Wabie had obviously underestimated her determination, and insulted her intelligence. Her reply, dated April 9, 1919, was predictable:

> Dear Sir
>
> I received your cheque April 5th and I am sending back. I nothing to do with North Temiskaming. My late mother

told me just before shes death to not go with my brothers and sister [to] North Temiskaming, and that time I was left all alone. I was only 16 years old and since that time I been paddle my own canoe. No one ever help me from North Temiskaming.

And I never signed my own name any Indian Band. Maybe they take my name not asking me. I am not belong to North Temiskaming band of Indians. I am New Ontario Indian woman. I was born Wabis Bay and that my late father left me his property - town of New Liskeard now and my grandfather's hunting lands from Cobalt up to Timmins. I want this government to pay me. I should get little share of my late father's lands.

Your truly
Nancy Wabi
Elk Lake

The next exchange on the subject took place three years later, in July, 1922, when W.H Lewis, Indian Agent at North Temiskaming, advised the Department that the Wabie family had renewed their fight to get compensation. The renewed interest came after the family read an article in the *New Liskeard Speaker* that mentioned the dispossession of the Wabie family from their land at New Liskeard.[20] *(New Liskeard Speaker, July 20, 1922: The article was actually an account of the founding of the Wabi Iron Works, a foundry established in 1907, and included some of the research on the Wabie family done by H.A. McEwan, the founder.)*

The article was entitled "Honest Indian," was illustrated with a drawing of an Indian in feathered headdress, and contained the following:

It is hard for any of us who now look upon Lake Temiskaming and visit the town of New Liskeard on the banks of the Wabi River to realize that these same regions a few years ago were a dense forest and the hunting grounds of a race now almost gone. The last of the race to occupy these regions was that of a tribe named Wabi, an Indian noted for his great strength and honesty. Selecting a hunting ground, he chose a site at the mouth of the river that now bears his name. Here he built a house for himself, made of logs, and in this he lived for several years, protected from the storm and cold, until the advent of the white man dispossessed him of his home and his hunting grounds.

With his canoe, fish nets, traps and gun, he paddled up and down the stream, harvesting the products of the forest and taking them across the lake to the "Hudson Bay Trading Post", bartering them for the necessities and comforts of life.

This giant scion of a noble race, the Algonquins, is gone, but here, in the spring of 1907, Messrs. H.A. McEwan and J.H. Lever founded on the bank of the Wabi, the first foundry and machine shop in the north.

In his letter to his superiors in Ottawa, Mr. Lewis, the Indian Agent in question stated that in his opinion, Joachim Wabigijik was "... just a squatter, and as soon as the white people came in he moved out."

The next exchange of correspondence came twelve years later, in 1934, when Nancy Wabie, now residing at Coral Rapids, Ontario (a settlement on the Abitibi River approximately half way between Fraserdale and Onakawana), wrote the Department of Indian Affairs, apparently in reply to a letter received by her in which the department informed her that she had no claim. Nancy Wabie did not marry, and had no children, and in 1934, she would have been 72 years old, but it is apparent that she was still combative. In her letter of September 4, 1934, she states:

"Your letter to hand of the 24th June, 1934 which you claim I have no interest in my father's property at New Liskeard where my father Joachim Wabikijik live for fifty years. I would like to get my money.

Gentlemen, I am not asking for Indian money. I am asking for what is coming to me for my father's property."

The final letter came in September 13, 1934, to Mr. Z. Caza, Indian Agent at Notre Dame du Nord.[21] *(Notre Dame du Nord was the name given to the former community of North Temiskaming. The community on the Indian Reserve retained the name North Temiskaming, while the community at what was previously known as Tête du Lac, Murray City, and North Temiscaming(ue), comprised of mostly French Canadians, became known by the new name. The two communities are approximately 1 km apart.)* in which A.F. MacKenzie, Secretary of the Department of Indian Affairs instructed Mr. Caza to inform Nancy Wabie that, "The Department has gone very fully into this matter, and finds that she has no valid claim either to the land or arrears of annuity." Typically, the letter was not addressed directly to Nancy Wabie, but to the Indian Agent, who presumably passed along the message.

Peter Hessel, author of *The Algonkin Tribe*[22] *(Peter Hessel,* The Algonkin Tribe: The Algonkins of the Ottawa Valley, An Historical Outline. *Arnprior, Ontario: Kichesippi Books, 1987.)* used this compensation claim as a research project while teaching a class in Algonquin history in 1989. A summary of some of the findings were reported in a series of articles in the *Temiskaming Speaker* in July 1989. Mr. Hessel summarized the case thus:

In spite of much legitimate evidence presented by Nancy Wabi over a period of 17 years, all levels of government refused to acknowledge her compensation claim for her ancestral property and hunting grounds. Notable is the absence of any suggestion by the authorities that Miss Wabi might wish to take her case to a court of law or an impartial board of inquiry. Clearly, her civil rights were violated. This case illustrates how native people were treated by government agencies during the first half of the 20th century.

In addition to the dismissive manner in which she was treated by the government authorities, one wonders why the several lawyers retained to plead her case were not able to get some satisfaction or at least get her case heard in a court of law."

26. Niven's accomplishments were often attributed to his rigorous work ethic and skilled management of his crews. Not only the success of the survey but also survival in the bush were dependent on strict discipline, and Niven would not have tolerated dissension.

27. Again, such a derogatory label was in keeping with 19th-century Anglo-Canadian language.

28. In 1869, the Canadian government approved the establishment of a post office at Fort Temiskaming. In turn, the Hudson's Bay Company began a mail service to other inland posts and to settlers of the area. Cassidy, *Arrow North*. 72

29. One chain = 66 feet.

30. Both the Canadian Temperance Union and its successor, the Dominion Alliance for the Total Suppression of the Liquor Traffic, worked vigorously for legislation to restrict the sale of liquor. This pressure finally resulted in the passing of the Canada Temperance Act of 1878, known as the Scott Act. It gave any part of the country the option of going dry if one-quarter of the electorate voted for it. Although prohibition was widely supported, disputes over the constitutionality of the act and the responsibility for its enforcement made application of the law difficult. Its main effect was to alienate the powerful liquor producers and further weaken the government's position with business and manufacturing interests. Kevin Knight, "Temperance Movements," *Catholic Encyclopedia, Vol. XIV*: online edition 1999, Available at: http://www.newadvent.org/cathen/14482a.htm, accessed May 23, 2001. Re-accessed March 11, 2004.

31. That there was mail delivery at all was remarkable. In the next year, postal centres would open at Baie-des-Pères and Farr's store at Humphrey's Depot (Haileybury). Fancy, *Temiskaming Treasure Trails*, 27.

32. This likely was Wright's Creek, originating in Quebec and joining the Blanche River part way through the Township of Casey, number 6.

33. In his notes Niven refers to this as Otter Creek. Niven, "Field Notes," 22.

34. In 19th-century Canada, Sunday was observed as a day of rest and church attendance. In the bush, workers would refrain from heavy work, but use the time to attend to necessary tasks such as equipment repairs, mending or the writing of letters.

35. A matter of opinion! The usually reticent Niven remarked in his field notes that "blackflies were out in full force." "Field Notes," 26.

36. Surveyors set stone posts into the ground to the surface level at important corners of their survey, providing a permanent and accurate record. Ladell, *They Made Their Mark*, 224.

37. Niven makes no comment about a discrepancy. He states that the line "east to the NE angle of Twp. 5 and boundary between Ontario and Quebec ... came out 26'84" [that is, 26 minutes, 84 seconds of latitude] north of 13 mile stone on Provincial boundary." Whatever questions may have arisen, Niven was confident of his own accuracy. *Ibid*, 26.

38. This was the same steamer *Argo* the party had used during the trip up the Ottawa to Temiskaming. Ten years later, the CPR would extend a branch from Mattawa to the head of Long Sault, a distance of some thirty miles, thus allowing travellers only a day's journey between Mattawa and Haileybury. This line, however, was to be eclipsed by the

Temiskaming and Northern Ontario Railway, finally completed in 1904, and running up the west side of the lake from North Bay. Fancy, *Temiskaming Treasure Trails*, 2-3, 111-112.

39. The Quebec Colonization Society Line was also known as the Lake Temiskaming Colonization Railway. It was a narrow gauge (36") railway constructed to bypass the Long Sault on the Ottawa River, utilizing small steamers to complete the voyage through to Mattawa. The engine arrived in August 1886, just in time for Niven's crew to make use of it. It was the precursor of the "Moccasin Line" which the CPR, as its new owner, would construct as far as Lake Kipawa in 1903. Tatley, *Northern Steamboat*, 77-78

40. In time and effort, this was a costly error. Those who went east via the CPR eventually reached Peterborough by 8:40 the following morning. From Nipissing Junction near Callander, the Northern Pacific Junction Railway ran to Gravenhurst. The Muskoka Junction Railway had been recently extended from Barrie to Huntsville at the southern end, and would have been the next rail link in his journey. Nick and Helma Mika, *An Illustrated History of Canadian Railways* (Belleville: Mika Publishing, 1986) 70.

41. La Vase was near the site of the historic portage linking the Mattawa River, Lake Nipissing and French River systems. The portage was well used during the time of Champlain by Native people and fur traders. Presently there are efforts to preserve this heritage trail for its archaeological and historical value. Michael Barnes, "Resurrecting a Long-gone Northern Portage," *Sudbury Star*, October 25, 1997.

Bibliography

Association of Ontario Land Surveyors (AOLS), Final Examination, Toronto, Ontario, February 1911.

_____, "Autobiographical Sketch of Alexander Niven, PLS, OLS," *Annual Report* Toronto, 1911, #26.

_____, "David Alexander Niven" (obituary). *Annual Report.* Toronto, 1924, #29.

Barnes, Michael, "Niven Always Got It done," *Sudbury Star*, November 26, 1996.

_____, "Resurrecting a Long-gone Northern Portage," *Sudbury Star*, October 25, 1997.

Bird, J. Brian, *The Natural Landscapes of Canada:A Study in Regional Earth Science.* 2nd ed. Toronto: John Wiley and Sons Canada, 1980.

Bonis, Robert R., ed., *A History of Scarborough.* Scarborough, Ontario: Scarborough Public Library, 1965.

Brander, Michael, *The Emigrant Scots.* London: Constable, 1982.

Cassidy, George L., *Arrow North: The Story of Temiskaming.* Cobalt, Ontario: Highway Book Shop, 1972.

Cowan, Helen I., *British Emigration to British North America: The First Hundred Years.* Toronto: University of Toronto Press, 1961.

Cummings, H.R., *Early Days in Haliburton.* Haliburton, Ontario:

Haliburton Heritage Museum, 1993. (Originally published by the Ontario Department of Lands and Forests, 1963.)

Dobrzensky, Leopolda z L., *Fragments of a Dream: Pioneering in Dysart Township and Haliburton Village*. Haliburton, Ontario: Municipality of Dysart, 1985.

Fancy, Peter, *Temiskaming Treasure Trails 1886-1903*. Cobalt, Ontario: Highway Bookshop, 1992.

Farr, C.C., *The Lake Temiskamingue District, Province of Ontario, Canada*. Toronto: Warwick Bros. & Rutter 1895.

De Fort-Menares, Anne M. *Canadian Pacific Railway Station: Mattawa, Ontario*. Hull, Quebec: Historic Sites and Monuments Board of Canada. RSR-174.

Gardner, H.F. *Nothing But Names: An Inquiry Into the Origin of the Names of the Counties and Townships of Ontario*. Toronto: George N. Morang and Co. Ltd., 1899.

Haliburton Village 1864-1964. Haliburton, Ontario: Rotary Club of Haliburton, 1964.

Hofstadter, Richard, William Miller and Daniel Aaron, *The American Republic, Volume 2: Since 1865*. Englewood Cliffs, New Jersey: Prentice-Hall, 1959.

Ladell, John L., *They Left Their Mark: Surveyors and Their Role in the Settlement of Ontario*. Toronto: Dundurn Press, 1993.

Land Settlement in New Ontario. (Prepared under the direction of Hon. E.J. Davis, Commissioner of Crown Lands.) Toronto: Warwick Bros. & Rutter, 1901; Archives of Ontario Pamphlet 1901 #13.

Lee, Robert C., *The Canada Company and the Huron Tract, 1826-1853: Personalities, Profits and Politics*. Toronto: Natural Heritage, 2004.

Mika, Nick, Helma Mika and Donald M. Wilson, *An Illustrated History of Canadian Railways*. Belleville: Mika Publishing Co., 1986.

Morel, Leo, *Mattawa: The Meeting of the Waters*. Mattawa, Ontario: Leo Morel and Société historique de Mattawa, 1980.

Niven, Alexander, "Accounts and Correspondence, 1887-88," Archives of Ontario, Crown Lands and Resources Records, RG-1-B-IV-Box 27.

_____, "Field Notes of Outline of Townships at the Head of Lake Temiscamingue 1886," Ministry of Natural Resources Survey Records, Peterborough, Ontario.

_____, "Miscellaneous Diaries and Records 1886-1898," Archives of Ontario, Crown Lands and Resources Records. RG1, CB1, reel 27.

Northern Districts of Ontario: Eastern Algoma, Northern Nipissing, Rainy River and Temiskaming. 2nd ed. (Prepared under instructions from Hon. A.S. Hardy, Commissioner of Crown Lands.) Toronto: Warwick Bros. & Rutter, 1895. Archives of Ontario Pamphlet, 1895 #20.

Quinsey, William J., ed., *Research Index of the Early Days of Land Surveying in Canada*, Vols. 1 and 2. Scarborough, Ontario: Association of Ontario Land Surveyors, 1992.

Robertson, James, "Surveys of Crown Lands in New Ontario." Association of Ontario Land Surveyors, 1904.

Sebert, L.M., "The Land Surveys of Ontario 1750-1980," *Cartographica*, 17, No.3 (1980).

Smart, Michael B., *The Role of the Land Surveyor in Geographic Feature and Place Naming in Ontario.* Scarborough, Ontario: Association of Ontario Land Surveyors, 1973.

Smout, T.C., *A Century of the Scottish People 1830-1950.* New Haven, Connecticut: Yale University Press, 1986.

Tatley, Richard, *Northern Steamboats: Timiskaming, Nipissing & Abitibi.* Erin, Ontario: Boston Mills Press, 1996.

Taylor, Bruce W., *A Centennial History of St. Andrew's Presbyterian Church, New Liskeard, Ontario, 1895-1995.* New Liskeard, Ontario: Privately published, 1995.

_____, *Leslie McFarlane: The Hardy Boys' Connection.* New Liskeard, Ontario: Haileybury Hardy Boys Committee, 1996.

_____, *New Liskeard: The Pioneer Years.* Cobalt, Ontario: Highway Book Shop, 2003.

_____, *Place Names of Temiskaming.* New Liskeard, Ontario: White Mountain Publications, 2000.

_____, *The Age of Steam on Lake Temiskaming.* Cobalt, Ontario: Highway Book Shop, 1993.

_____, *The Plaunt Family of Renfrew: A History*. New Liskeard, Ontario: Privately published, 1991.

_____, *Two Gaelic Soldiers: A Story of Two Canadian Pioneer Families*. Atikokan, Ontario: Quetico Publishing, 1978.

_____, *Steep Rock: The Men and the Mines*. Atikokan, Ontario: Quetico Publishing, 1978.

Theriault, Madeline Katt, *Moose to Moccasins: The Story of Ka Kita Wa Pa No Kwe*. Toronto: Natural Heritage, 1992.

Therrien, G., *Mattawa: Our Timeless Town*. Société historique de Mattawa Historical Society. Manuscript submitted for publishing 1999.

Weaver, W.F., "Ontario Surveys and the Land Surveyor," *Canadian Geographical Journal*, 1946.

Wilson, Donald M., *The Ontario and Quebec Railway: A History of the Development of the Canadian Pacific System in Southern Ontario*. Belleville: Mika Publishing Co., 1984.

Wilson, Hap, *Rivers of the Upper Ottawa Valley*. Hyde Park, Ontario: Canadian Recreational Canoeing Association, 1993.

Index

Belleville and North Hastings Railway, 32

Bernard, Joseph (Bernard Naraseau), 5, 73, 94, 113

Berriedale, 74

Berthoaume, Flavienne, see Flavienne Piche

Bird, J. Brian, 99

Blanche River, 4, 19, 52, 54-56, 63, 69, 70, 83, 85, 98, 121, 130

Blind Institute (Brantford), 103

Bolger, Francis, 111

Bonin, Joseph, 122, 124

Borden, Robert (Sir) (Prime Minister), 125, 139

Botham, Thomas H., 32, 44

Bowman, C.D., 103

Brantford, City of, 103, 108

Brethour, Township of, 54, 59, 61, 95

Britain, see Great Britain

British Canadian Power Company, 124

Bruton, Township of, 93

Buffalo (New York), 88

Bucke, Richard Maurice (Dr.), 103

Bucke, Township of (Township of #1), 45, 50, 95, 103, 109, 110, 121, 122

Bullock, Loretta, see Loretta Heard

Burford, Village of, 108

Burwash, Adam, 138, 116, 119

Burwash, Elizabeth (Piche) (Mrs. Adam), 116, 119, 120, 138

Cabedia territory, 130

Cadestral surveys, 29, 111

Callander, Town of, 72, 76

Calydor Hospital (Gravenhurst), 139

Canada Company, 14

Canada Temperance Act (1878), see also Scott Act, 57

Canadian Land and Emigration Company (CLTE), 13, 14, 93, 103

Canadian Pacific Railway (CPR), 14, 18, 23, 24, 32, 35, 36, 73, 74, 79, 85, 95, 101, 111, 113

Canadian Pacific Railway Station: Mattawa, Ontario, 35, 36

Canadian Shield, 19, 24

Canadian Temperance Union, 144

Caribbean, 88

Carleton Junction, 35, 79

Carr, Margaret, see Margaret Heard

Carr, W.S., 133, 134
Casey, Township of, 60, 61, 95
Cassidy, George L., 115
Cat, see also Katt:
    Augustus, 131
    Angelline (Mrs. Machelle),
    131
    Machelle, 131
    Mathew, 131
    Terrance, 131
Caticumni River (Wahnaby's
    Creek), 51, 83
Caza, Z. (Indian Agent), 143
Census of 1871, 12
Central America, 88
Charlton Cemetery, 109
Charlton, Village of, 100, 108,
    109
Cholera, 9, 10
Chromate, Betsi, see Betsi Wabi
Church of Scotland, 92
Clay Belt, 29, 82, 98
Clyde, Township of, 93
Cobalt Lake, 22
Cobalt, Town of, 99, 109, 110,
    115, 120, 124, 129, 136, 140
Coburg, Town of, 103
Cochrane, Town of, 30, 95, 98
Colonization Roads, 23
Commissioner of Crown
    Lands, see E.J. Davis
Coral Rapids, Village of, 142
Coster, ___ (Mr.), 43, 115

Cree First Nation, 16
Cromarty (Scotland), 9, 91, 92
Crops, 82, 83
Crown Lands Department, 14,
    24, 25, 44, 87, 100, 104
Cuba, 88
Cunningham family, 75

Davis, E.J. (Hon.) (Crown
    Lands Commissioner), 105
Dawson, George, 130
Dawson Point, see also Wabi
    Point, 127, 130
Deep River, Town of, 127
Deleage, ___ (Rev. Father), 119
Department of Indian Affairs
    (Federal), 117, 118, 136,
    138-141, 142, 143
Department of Lands and
    Forests, 105, 138
Des Joachim Dam (Swishaw
    Dam), 127
Des Qunize River, 19
Dingman, S. (Inspector), 117
Dominion Alliance for the
    Total Suppression of the
    Liquor Traffic, 144
Don Mills, Village of, 10
Don River, 10
Dudley, Township of, 93
Duhamel, Bishop, 127
Duhamel, Township of, 123
Dumoine River, 115

Guilford, Township of, 93
Guillet, Paul, 95

Haileybury School of Mines, 110
Haileybury, Town of, 22, 31, 41, 102-105, 110, 121, 123, 124, 129, 130, 132, 135, 138, 145
Haliburton, District of, 88, 93, 114
Haliburton, Town of, 12, 14, 93-95, 99, 100, 103
Haliburton, Provisional County of, 14, 15, 94, 102, 109
Haliburton, Sarah (Mrs. T.C.), 93
Haliburton, Thomas Chandler (Hon.), 13, 93
Hamilton, ___ (Chief Factor), 116
Harburn, Township of, 93
Harcourt, Township of, 93
Harley Line, 22
Harley, Township of, 52, 95
Harrington, Amos, 88
Harrington, Mary Jane, see Mary Jane Telfer
Harris, Township of, 95, 130
Hartfell, 75
Havelock, Township of, 93
Heard:
    Allan, 109

Andrew, 103, 109
Arthur, 109
Arvilla (Latchford) (Mrs. Irvin), 100, 108, 109
Emma, see Emma Tripp
Everett, 99, 102-104, 108
Irvin, 99, 100, 102-109
James (Hurd), 31, 44, 46, 58, 68, 103, 108
James A., 109
Jane (Rutherford) (Mrs. Rob Roy), 102
Jane (Sawyer) (Mrs. Joseph), 109
Joseph, 31, 44, 58, 68, 109
Loretta (Bullock) (Mrs. William Robert), 103, 109
Margaret (Carr) (Mrs. James), 109
Maria (Fernholm) (Mrs. Rob Roy), 109
Osborne, 108
Rob Roy, 102
Rob Roy (son of Joseph), 109
William, 15, 109
William Robert, 15, 103, 109
Height of Land, 19
Herkes, Janet, see Janet Telfer
Hessel, Peter, 143
Hill, Clark & Francis (planing mill), 108
Hilliard, Township of, 54, 59, 95

Morin, Alfred, 116

Morin, Annie (Piche) (Mrs. Alfred), 116

Morrison, Ann, see Ann Niven

Mourier, Father, 129

Mount Vernon, Town of, 108

Mowat, Oliver (Premier), 94

Muir, Alexander, 92

Muir, John, 11, 92

Murray City, 116, 143

Murray, Thomas, 115, 116, 122

Murray, William, 99, 100, 102, 104, 105, 115

Muskoka, District of, 35, 83, 88, 107

Muskoka Junction Railway, 4, 74, 76, 146

Narrows, the, 40, 114

Naraseau, Bernard, see Joe Bernard

Native Peoples, 16, 21, 41, 101, 116, 119, 126, 129, 133, 139, 146

Nedelec, Father, 127

New Liskeard Agricultural College, 108

New Liskeard Speaker, 105, 108, 141

New Liskeard, Town of, 52, 99, 100, 103, 105-109, 120, 123, 125-130, 133, 135-137, 141, 142

New Ontario, 12, 102, 136, 137

New York, State of, 96

Niagara Escarpment, 122

Niagara Falls, Town of, 87, 88

Niagara Grammar School, 13

Niagara-on-the-Lake (UC), 12

Nipissing, District of, 4, 16

Nipissing Junction, 146

Niven, Alexander, 4, 12-16, 24, 25, 29, 31, 32, 36, 39, 40, 42, 44-46, 56-61, 64, 68, 71, 79. 87, 94, 95, 111, 113, 114, 121, 122, 124, 144, 146

Niven, Ann (Morrison) (Mrs. Robert), 12

Niven, David, 12

Niven, Maggie (McEvoy) (Mrs. Alexander), 13, 14

Niven, Robert, 12

Niven's Meridian, 15, 30, 95

Noranda (Quebec), 120

North Bay, City of, 120, 146

North Bay Public Library, 135

North Temiskaming, see also Tête du Lac, 128, 129, 134, 135, 137, 138, 140, 141

North Temiskaming Band, 126, 128, 129, 134, 135, 138, 140

North Temiskaming Reserve, 128, 132, 137, 138, 143

North York (Ontario), 44, 75

Northern Ontario, 3

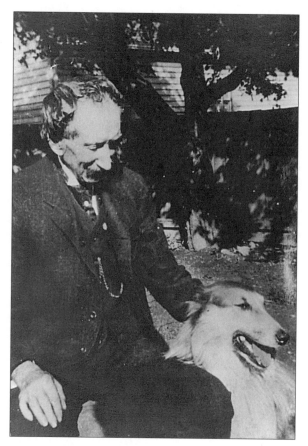

Alexander Herkes Telfer with his dog Colonel.
Courtesy of Lorene DiCorpo.